THE JOSSEY-BASS ACADEMIC ADMINISTRATOR'S GUIDE TO

Budgets and Financial Management

The Jossey-Bass Academic Administrator's Guides are designed to help new and experienced campus professionals when a promotion or move brings on new responsibilities, new tasks, and new situations. Each book focuses on a single topic, exploring its application to the higher education setting. These real world guides provide advice about day-to-day responsibilities as well as an orientation to the organizational environment of campus administration. From department chairs to office staff supervisors, these concise resources will help college and university administrators understand and overcome obstacles to success.

We hope you will find this volume useful in your work. To that end, we welcome your reaction to this volume and to the series in general, including suggestions for future topics.

THE JOSSEY-BASS

ACADEMIC ADMINISTRATOR'S
GUIDE TO

Budgets and Financial Management

MARGARET J. BARR

JOSSEY-BASS
A Wiley Imprint
www.josseybass.com

Published by Jossey-Bass
A Wiley Imprint
989 Market Street, San Francisco, CA 94103-1741   www.josseybass.com

Jossey-Bass books and products are available through most bookstores. To contact Jossey-Bass directly call our Customer Care Department within the U.S. at 800-956-7739, outside the U.S. at 317-572-3986 or fax 317-572-4002.

Jossey-Bass also publishes its books in a variety of electronic formats. Some content that appears in print may not be available in electronic books.

Library of Congress Cataloging-in-Publication Data

Barr, Margaret J.
    Jossey-Bass academic administrator's guide to budgets and financial management/
Margaret J. Barr.—1st ed.
        p. cm.
Includes bibliographical references and index.
    ISBN 0-7879-5957-X (alk. paper)
    1. Education, Higher—United States—Finance—Handbooks, manuals, etc.
    2. Universities and colleges—United States—Business management—Handbooks, manuals, etc.
    I. Title: Academic administrator's guide to budgets and financial management.
    II. Jossey-Bass, Inc. III. Title.
    LB2342 .B325 2002
    378.1'06—dc21

                                                                        2002010334

Printed in the United States of America
FIRST EDITION
PB Printing   10 9 8 7 6 5 4 3 2 1

CONTENTS

PREFACE

MOST PROGRAM MANAGERS, principal investigators, division leaders, and department chairs are bright, capable, and competent persons in their field of expertise. However, when appointments are made to administrative posts in higher education, new academic managers often come to their positions without much experience in fiscal management and administration. Prior to their appointment, the personal interactions of new academic managers with the fiscal management of the institution have primarily related to individual issues regarding salaries, benefits, and grants. An administrative role, however, carries with it expectations for effective management of the fiscal resources of the department or unit. Questions that must be answered are varied and will be asked of the new budget manager very quickly. Can a new piece of equipment be purchased? Is it possible to immediately hire a new support staff person for the unit? Will the department provide travel support for a faculty member to attend a conference and present a paper? The list of questions could go on and on. It is no wonder that a new budget manager can feel a bit overwhelmed. Where can you, as a new budget manager, find the answers to questions that you and others have, and how can you sort out the real fiscal issues within your unit?

This volume is designed to provide initial assistance to new budget managers. In order to become effective as a budget manager you must first understand the context for decision making within the institution. Chapter One lays the foundation for understanding budgeting and fiscal management. It defines terms, discusses the role of the unit budget in detail, and provides a discussion of the fiscal context of higher education. In addition, Chapter One focuses on the sources of financial support for higher education and the differences between public and private (independent) institutions. Understanding the broad fiscal context faced by the institution contributes to academic managers' mastery of their specific role and function within the institution.

Chapter Two discusses the purposes of budgets and the elements of a budget. Chapter Three discusses in detail the budget cycles that must be dealt with by a unit budget manager. It presents the steps of the budget process from initial budget development through analysis of fiscal performance. It also discusses the operating budget, the capital budget, and auxiliary budgets.

Chapter Four describes the pitfalls and problems faced by unit budget managers and suggests how to avoid such problems. This compilation of problems and strategies is the result of interviews with fiscal managers at several kinds of institutions.

Although loss of resources is never easy, it can occur. Chapter Five focuses on the unique issues related to budget reductions and presents strategies to deal with such issues. Each chapter provides guided questions to relate the material to the specific setting faced by the new academic budget manager. The volume includes a glossary of useful terms related to budgeting and fiscal management. Finally, the book provides a list of suggested readings.

WHO SHOULD READ THIS VOLUME?

Whether you are a new department chair, a principal investigator on a large research grant, or a new director of a business, academic support, or student affairs unit, you will need to create, defend, and manage a budget. Effectiveness in your new administrative role depends, in part, on your understanding the financial issues influencing your institution and your unit. Understanding the "big picture" is essential to effectively present your unit priorities, needs, and aspirations during the development, review, and approval of your unit budget requests. Success in matters related to fiscal management also depends on establishing the critical link between unit needs and institutional priorities. Finally, your success as a budget manager depends on your ability to articulate both the short- and long-term fiscal and service implications for new programs, expanded services, new equipment, new facilities, and increased staff or staff reductions.

The volume focuses on practical issues of budget and fiscal management and is designed to specifically aid new budget managers. Budgeting and fiscal management are but one part of your new duties. However, understanding and mastering budgeting and fiscal management is essential for your success.

This book will also be useful to graduate students and entry-level professionals contemplating administrative responsibilities in the future.

LIMITATIONS OF THE VOLUME

This volume provides general information about the budget process and does not attempt to deal in depth with any single issue facing a unit budget manager. It will help illuminate common problems and solutions and help readers gain confidence in broad areas of financial issues. The book does not extend into the extremely complex and critical areas of legal and personnel policy that are so often linked to the financial aspects of academic management. The author strongly advises all academic budget managers to consult with their campus legal counsel and personnel officers with regard to decisions requiring these special kinds of expertise.

ACKNOWLEDGMENTS

Even though I am the sole author of this volume, I have not written it "alone": my work has evolved through my education and experience. A number of people have helped shape my thoughts and approaches to solving problems and providing information. My thanks go to David Brightman and Gale Erlandson who encouraged me to write this book. Their support over the years that I have written for Jossey-Bass has been invaluable. I am also grateful to the superb editorial staff at Jossey-Bass whose patience and guidance have taught me to be a better writer.

I would also like to thank the patient folks in the budget and finance offices of six institutions where I worked (State University of New York at Binghamton, Trenton State College [now the College of New Jersey], the University of Texas at Austin, Northern Illinois University, Texas Christian University, and Northwestern University). They helped me learn about budgets, financing of higher education, and my role in that process. In particular, I would like to acknowledge John Pembroke from Northern Illinois University, E. Leigh Secrest from Texas Christian University, and James Elsass from Northwestern University for careful tutelage and help when I needed it most. I am grateful for their time and patience.

In addition, Eric Wachtel and Eugene Sunshine from Northwestern University provided a number of insights as I was writing this volume. Each of them gave generously of their time. Their perspectives help shape the content of this volume and the utility it will have for academic budget managers.

My family and friends always support me when I take on a project such as this, and I am grateful. Finally, I would like to thank Vadal Redmond and George McClellan for their assistance in creating this manuscript.

ABOUT THE AUTHOR

MARGARET J. BARR served as vice president for student affairs at Northwestern University from October 1992 until July 2000 when she retired. She currently is professor emeritus in the School of Education and Social Policy at Northwestern and is engaged in part-time consulting and volunteer work. Dr. Barr was vice chancellor for student affairs at Texas Christian University for eight years prior to her appointment at Northwestern. She served as vice president for student affairs at Northern Illinois University from 1982 to 1985 and was assistant vice president for student affairs at that same institution from 1980 to 1982. She was first assistant and then associate dean of students at the University of Texas at Austin from 1971 to 1980. She has also served as director of housing and director of the college union at Trenton State College and assistant director and director of women's residences at the State University of New York at Binghamton.

In her various administrative roles, Barr has always carried responsibility for supervision of operating budgets. During her eighteen years as a vice president, she supervised operating budgets for both general revenue and auxiliary enterprises of up to $70 million. She has been involved in capital projects including construction of new residence halls, new recreation facilities, new dining facilities, and a multicultural center/academic advising center. She has supervised major repair and renovation projects covering multiple years at three institutions.

She has held numerous leadership positions with the American College Personnel Association (ACPA), including a term as president (l983–1984). She has been the recipient of the ACPA Contribution to Knowledge Award (1990) and Professional Service Award (1986) and was an ACPA Senior Scholar from 1986 to 1991.

She also has been active in the National Association of Student Personnel Administrators (NASPA), including service as the director of the NASPA Institute for Chief Student Affairs Officers (1989, 1990) and the NASPA Foundation Board. She has just completed a two-year term as president of the NASPA Foundation Board. Barr was the recipient of the NASPA Outstanding Contribution to Literature and Research Award in 1986, the award for Outstanding Contribution to Higher Education in 2000, and was named a Pillar of the Profession by NASPA in that same year.

She is the author or editor of numerous books and monographs, including *The Handbook for Student Affairs Administration* (1993), co-editor of the second edition of *The Handbook for Student Affairs Administration* (2000) with M. Desler, co-editor of *New Futures for Student Affairs* with M. Lee Upcraft (1990), the editor of *Student Services and the Law* (1988), and co-editor of *Developing Effective Student Services Programs: A Guide for Practitioners* with L. A. Keating (1985). She served as editor-in-chief for the monograph series *New Directions for Student Services* from 1986 to 1998. She is also the author of numerous book and monograph chapters.

Barr received a bachelor's degree in elementary education from the State University College at Buffalo, Buffalo, New York in 1961 and a master's degree in college student personnel-higher education from Southern Illinois University-Carbondale in 1964. She received a Ph.D. in educational administration from the University of Texas at Austin in 1980.

THE JOSSEY-BASS ACADEMIC ADMINISTRATOR'S GUIDE TO

Budgets and Financial Management

Money, Money, Money

BUDGETS AND FINANCIAL MATTERS never seem to be topics that stir the souls of new academic managers. However, understanding both the budgetary processes and the sources of institutional financial support will be essential for your success and that of your department or program. As a manager in higher education, one of your primary roles is to garner the resources needed to implement the ideas, programs, services, and needed classes and instruction required or desired by your students, your colleagues, and other constituent groups. And it is not enough to merely obtain money to support the unit. You also need to assure that those resources are spent in accordance with institutional guidelines as well as state and federal law. Remember that in order for goals and objectives to be reached, the needed human and fiscal resources must be in place, and that means mastering budgeting and financial issues.

THE ROLE OF THE BUDGET MANAGER

The organization of each institution of higher education is unique. Some complex institutions have an elaborate organization with many program and administrative units. Other institutions are organized in a less complex fashion. No matter what the organization of the institution or the specific title of the unit budget manager (program manager, director, chair, or department head), the roles of the unit budget manager are very consistent.

First is the fiscal role of the unit budget manager, which will discussed throughout this volume. The financial success of the institution is highly dependent on unit budget managers' exercising sound fiduciary responsibility. That is not usually an easy task, for the pressures are many and the issues are complex. But unit budget managers are expected to follow institutional fiscal policies and solve problems before they become major concerns for the institution.

A second role, less recognized than the fiscal role of unit budget managers, is that of listening post for the institution. It is often unit budget managers who hear of issues and problems influencing employee morale or their ability to get work done. For example, a unit budget manger is often the first person to hear of or personally experience problems with a new purchasing system. If the unit budget manager just assumes that those individuals responsible for the installation and maintenance of the new purchasing system are aware of the problem, the system problem may never be addressed and the situation will not get any better. The wise unit budget manager conveys specific concerns to others within the institution who can address the issue and offers to partner with them in an improvement effort. To illustrate, the unit budget manager could provide specific examples of the problems she experiences or run a test purchase order on the system so the actual problem can be identified. The involvement is well worth the effort and reduces frustration for everyone involved.

A third function of the unit budget manager focuses on resource gathering through fund-raising. The unit budget manager helps those within the unit coordinate requests for external support with the development office or officer. In addition, they assist members of the unit in identifying possible funding sources for their idea or program. Finally, unit budget managers indirectly serve as friend-makers for the institution in their interactions with vendors and members of the public. One development officer noted, in casual conversation, that everyone in the institution has the potential to be a fundraiser, but they rarely recognize their role in that process.

A fourth role of the unit budget manager is designated problem solver for the unit when it comes to fiscal issues. It is the unit budget manger who must figure out how to approach a problem and gain an optimal solution for the unit. This requires development of a web of helping relationships within the institution. Understanding who to call under what circumstances is a prime role of the unit budget manager. It is clear that a unit budget manager deals with much more than money and balance sheets.

DEFINITION OF TERMS

Throughout this volume a number of terms will be used interchangeably. The broadest definition possible has been developed for terms so that the volume can be useful to individuals in all types of institutions. In addition to the glossary provided at the end of the volume, the following definitions of terms will be helpful in understanding this volume.

Unit Budget Manager or Academic Budget Manager

A unit budget manager is someone with administrative responsibility for a financial account or a number of financial accounts within the institution. For purposes of this volume, a unit budget manager could be a department chair with responsibility for accounts associated with a specific academic department, or a director with responsibility for a center or support unit. Finally, a unit budget manager could be a program director or principal investigator with responsibility for management of a grant or a discrete program unit. The unit budget manager may be assisted in his budget and fiscal management role by other staff members, but the ultimate fiduciary responsibility rests with the unit budget manager.

Unit

A unit can be any administrative division of the institution including a small discrete program. For example, for purposes of this volume, a budget unit may be a small department, a specific program, a research grant, or a division of the institution. The principles of budget and fiscal management remain the same.

Budget Office

In large and complex institutions, there may be a well-developed budget office with professional staff assigned to provide assistance to major budget units within the college or university. In smaller institutions, the resources are usually more restricted, with a small central staff providing support, and reliance is on the expertise of a few people. Whatever the organization, when the term *central budget office* is used in this volume, it refers to the entity that oversees all budget or fiscal operations within the institution.

For other terms please check the glossary of terms at the end of this volume.

THE BIG PICTURE

As an effective academic budget manager you will seek to understand the larger fiscal context of higher education and the influence that context may have on institutional budget priorities and ultimately unit budgets. You must also be able to identify the sources of the funds used to support your unit activities and the limitations that may be placed on budget decisions because of the fund source. Basic understanding of these broad fiscal issues helps you as academic budget manager ask intelligent questions, potentially identify new sources of support for unit objectives, and strengthen your ability to communicate unit needs to fiscal decision makers both within and without the institution.

Imagine that you are the president of Alpha University and are dealing with issues of budget. A combination of factors has resulted in a net revenue increase for the institution of approximately $10 million for the next fiscal year. The revenue increase is the result of an increase in tuition and fees, modest enrollment growth at the undergraduate level, new gifts to support the establishment of three endowed chairs resulting in additional funds being available for redistribution, and a modest growth in research grants resulting in an increase in indirect cost reimbursement. The issue for you and the institutional budget committee is to decide how best to invest these new resources within the institution.

Increases in budget requests for the next fiscal year from academic and support units total $14 million. Although it is clear that all such requests cannot be funded, the question of how to allocate the new revenue is much more complex than simply denying funding to $4 million of requests. Issues that influence the allocation of the $10 million in additional revenue include:

A governing board policy requires that any increase in tuition and fees results in a proportional increase in the student financial aid budget (estimated cost: $1 million).

The faculty and staff expect at least a 3.5 percent salary increment for the next fiscal year (estimated cost: $1.6 million).

Health insurance premiums have skyrocketed, resulting in a premium increase for the next fiscal year (estimated cost: $650,000 for the institutional share).

After a Title IX complaint an agreed-upon plan with the Office of Civil Rights involves an increase in support for women's intercollegiate athletics (estimate cost: $350,000 next fiscal year and an additional $200,000 per year for the next five years).

New faculty must be hired for the next academic year to convert the increased demand for required core courses in the liberal arts college. Students have been unable to get into needed courses in a timely manner (estimated cost: $500,000 increase in the base budget).

An unanticipated increase in postal rates results in an increase in the base budget for next year (estimate cost: $50,000).

The first phase of a five-year upgrade of the network and supporting software must begin (estimated cost $500,000.).

The governing board would like to attract more National Merit Scholars and has strongly suggested that money be designated in the institutional base budget for that purpose (estimated cost: $250,000 in the first year).

As Figure 1.1 demonstrates, the actual amount of money available to fund increased budget requests from academic and support units has been drastically reduced due to the list of mandated cost increases. Less than 50 percent of the original $10 million in new revenue is available to support budget requests from academic and support units. In addition, the president has several new initiatives that she believes are critical in order to move the institution forward. None of the priorities of the president are included in the $14 million of budget increase requests already under consideration. If the presidential priorities were to be added, another $5 million of requests would be on the table for consideration. It is clear with only slightly over $5 million available and requests totaling $19 million dollars that many worthy programs and activities will not receive budget support in the next fiscal year. Such dilemmas are not rare in higher education. The wise budget manager must understand these kinds of realities and prepare budget requests insofar as possible to meet institutional goals.

The next section presents an overview of the fiscal context of higher education and a review of the multiple sources of financial support for the higher education enterprise. The similarities and differences between public and private institutions with regard to fiscal matters are also discussed. Finally, the chapter concludes with a brief discussion about why all of this is important to a new budget manager within the educational enterprise.

Figure 1.1. Alpha University's Distribution of New Revenue of $10 Million for the Next Fiscal Year.

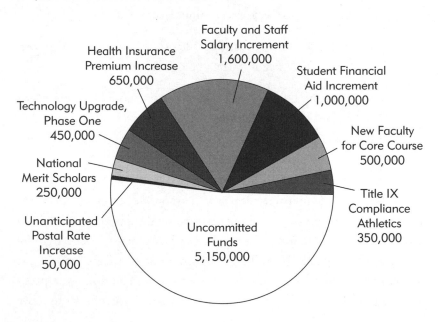

THE FISCAL CONTEXT
OF HIGHER EDUCATION

Higher education institutions, whether public or private, are experiencing great changes related to identifying and capturing resources to support the enterprise. The broader fiscal context of higher education sets very real constraints on what can and what cannot be accomplished in any institution of higher education. These broader fiscal issues include growing competition for funds in both the public and private sector, concerns about the rising costs of higher education, increased regulations including a rise in unfunded federal and state mandates, increased competition for a skilled workforce from business and industry, the growth of technology, and the rising costs for the purchase of goods and services.

Increased Competition for Funds

Competition for funds has increased in recent years and is likely to continue to do so in the future. In most states, state government has become a growth industry; the number and variety of programs funded out of tax support grows each year. In addition, some state programs, such as health care, have expanded in order to meet the needs of an aging population. Other programs, such as prisons and public safety, have grown because of an increase in volume and public demands. Streets and highways need to be rebuilt or expanded. Recreational use of forest preserves, beaches, parks, and other state land has grown. The list of state needs goes on and on. Suffice it to say that higher education is but one of many programs seeking support from a limited amount of money at the state level (Schuh, 2000). The result has been less and less direct support for public institutions of higher education and increased expectations that such institutions develop new ways to get the resources necessary to operate the enterprise. In fact, some public institutions have changed their rhetoric and describe their institution as state "related" rather than state "supported" because the contribution of the state to the institution has diminished so much. The reduction in available state funding also influences private higher education in both direct and indirect ways. For example, state financial support to individual students can be used by the student at both public and private institutions. If funding for such programs is reduced or remains steady, more of the burden for individual student aid is shifted to the institution from the state.

During the last decade, many public institutions have joined private institutions in seeking support from foundations, alumni, parents, friends, businesses, and industry. Billion-dollar campaigns are no longer unusual. Concurrently, other charitable institutions have increased their quest for funding support. Competition for private funds is fierce and likely to remain so in the near future. Fund-raising has become a major enterprise for many institutions, and annual fund-raising is becoming essential to institutional success.

In addition, both public and private institutions have expanded their services to include specialized grants and contracts with business, industry, and government. Indirect cost recovery from such grants and contracts has become a major revenue source for many institutions. Competition is great in this domain and is likely to be so in the future.

Cost Concerns

The cost of attendance at institutions of higher education, both public and private, is becoming a growing societal concern. Parents, legislators, alumni, and friends are all expressing reservations about the rising costs of tuition, fees, room, and board. Development of new student fees as a method to garner resources had been popular with many institutions in the past. But with cost issues of concern, new fees are instituted much less frequently than in the previous decade.

The issues related to cost of attendance are also directly linked to financial aid for students. Access and choice have been central to the mission of many public and private institutions. In order to support an economically diverse student body, the federal and state governments and institutions have invested heavily in financial aid to students. The grants and loans from federal and state governments do not meet the full cost of attendance at most institutions and must be supplemented by institutional funds or endowment income to support additional financial aid. As the cost of attendance rises, so do financial aid budgets, and the resources of the institution are stretched. The problem is compounded in institutions with graduate education programs. In such environments, the cost of instruction and research is high and the payment by students for such educational access is relatively low. Cost and financial aid issues will be part of the fiscal future of higher education in the United States for years to come.

Increased Regulations and Unfunded Mandates

Within the last fifty years, American higher education has experienced a great increase in regulation from both the state and federal governments. Many of these statutory requirements or agency regulations require additional expense to achieve compliance. However, funding for compliance at either the state or federal level has not been forthcoming. To illustrate, the Animal Welfare Act (AWA) (70 U.S.C. sec. 2131 et. seq.) has a number of specific regulations regarding the care of animals used in research; if the institution is not in compliance with the regulations, research funding may be withheld. The Occupational Safety and Health Act of 1970 (OSHA) (29 U.S.C. sec. 651 et. seq.) provides regulations governing everything from disposal of contaminated materials to the configuration of work stations. The Family Education Rights and Privacy Act (FERPA or the Buckley Amendment) (34 CFR 99) regulates directory information and provides privacy protection for students. The Human Subjects Research Act (45 CFR 46) requires disclosure and monitoring of human subjects in research studies. The Student Right-to-Know and Campus Security Act (20 U.S.C. 1092[f]) requires notification of crime statistics and other data on an annual basis. These statutes are just examples of the maze of federal and state regulations that must be complied with at any college or university. All have financial implications and require human and financial resources to comply. The regulatory context is one that must be constantly monitored to reduce both the fiscal and human impact of such regulations on institutional operations.

Competition for Faculty and Staff

Higher education is actively competing with business and industry for both skilled and unskilled workers. That has not always been the case, but in a robust economy wages and benefits in business and industry can far outstrip those provided at both public and private higher education institutions. The problem of attracting and retaining staff members has become even more difficult with the advent of technology. Both technical managers and technical support staff are in high demand in all sectors of the economy. And the problem of attracting and retaining personnel is not limited to staff ranks. New doctoral candidates and young faculty members are also being heavily recruited by business and industry.

While institutions try to attract and retain new faculty and staff, they must assure that those individuals who are currently a part of the work force are not disadvantaged by any scheme to attract new hires. Failure to develop a reasonable approach to unacceptable rates of turnover will result in increased cost and frustration. New compensation schemes are being developed at some institutions to address the problem, as well as new and more attractive benefits packages. Whatever the approach, this issue is likely to have huge financial implications for institutions.

Competition for Students

Competition for students is growing, particularly with regard to minority student enrollments. Some institutions are absolutely dependent on enrollment to cover the cost of operations for the fiscal year. The loss of even twenty students can mean the difference, at those institutions, between institutional fiscal failure and success. For other institutions, the budget is not as enrollment driven, but issues of access and choice, referenced earlier, remain at the forefront of fiscal decisions. Competition for students results in higher financial aid budgets and other tuition discounting schemes such as a lower rate for a second child from the same family. But financial aid is often not enough to attract the students desired by institutions, and money is being focused on amenities that make the institution more inviting to prospective students. Finally, the cost of the actual recruitment process continues to grow as each institution attempts to get a specific message out to students and their parents.

In addition to recruitment efforts for traditionally aged students, many institutions have sought new markets for their educational programs by embracing adult and returning students. Creation of education and support programs for nontraditional students is not an inexpensive undertaking. With new markets come new demands for services. It is a volatile, changing, and risky environment, and the costs associated with recruitment and retention of students will grow each year.

Cost of Technology

Technology is both a blessing and a curse for institutions of higher education. It is a blessing because it provides new tools for communication and research. Communication is more rapid and access to information has grown geometrically. It is a curse for a number of reasons, but for the purposes of this discussion the focus is on the fiscal implications of the use of technology on campuses. In a rapidly evolving environment, technological innovations are installed at great cost and seem to become outdated before the installation is even complete. The costs of networking a campus and maintaining the technology infrastructure are enormous, as are the costs of replacing personal computers to keep up with the latest changes in hardware and software.

In addition, technology has brought with it the power to change the ways an institution does business. Many colleges and universities are in the process of developing new student information systems, as well as systems to deal with accounting, purchasing, and human resource management. Each of these new systems has a price tag for both initial installation and then maintenance of the system. For many years, there was hope that positions could be eliminated as a result of technology; that has not proven to be the case. There are many good reasons for installing technological innovations on a college campus. Saving money is not one of them.

Rising Cost of Goods and Services

Higher education has certainly not been immune from inflation. The cost for goods and services purchased by institutions increases each year. At a large institution, minute increases in the cost of utilities, for example, can have great budget implications because of the volume needed to meet institutional needs. Costs in all sectors of goods and services have risen and must be paid by the institution. Only an examination of the way business is done within the institution will stop the cost for goods and services from spiraling out of control. For example, questions must be asked whether there are energy-saving measures that can be instituted that pay for themselves within two years. Are there less expensive ways to communicate with parents and students? Creative solutions are needed for these and other questions (see Exhibit 1.1).

WHERE DOES THE MONEY COME FROM?

A number of fund sources support both public and private (independent) institutions of higher education. The emphasis and dependence on each source of financial support will vary between institutions even of the same type. However, the greatest variance in sources of support will occur between public and private institutions, although some observers say that those distinctions are becoming more blurred in the changing financial environment of higher education.

Exhibit 1.1. Questions to Consider Regarding the Budget Implications for Your Unit.

1. What constraints from the larger environment will influence your daily work as an academic budget manager?
2. What are the potential opportunities for your unit because of events and decisions within the larger environment?
3. Does your unit have any budgetary responsibility for the financial support of graduate and undergraduate students? If so, how much money is involved?
4. Is your unit responsible for responding to unfunded federal and state mandates? If so, what are the budget implications for this fiscal year and beyond?
5. Is your unit finding it difficult to fill support and technical staff positions? If so, why?
6. Does your unit hold fiscal responsibility for installation, upgrades, and replacement of computer equipment and software? Is the budget sufficient for the needs?

State Appropriated Funds

Funds from the state government are the primary source of income for most public colleges and universities. At a community college such income may also be supplemented by direct support from the county or municipality where the institution is located.

The process involved in allocating state funds to an institution of higher education will differ in each state. Some states use formula funding based on the number of full-time, part-time, graduate, and undergraduate students, with different funding for each student category. In other states, formula funding is based on a rolling average of credit hours produced over the last five years by the institution. In still other states, legislative review of the institutional budget is extensive and may involve line item review of all budget items. Some states use a combination of formula funding (overseen by the higher education agency within the state) and extensive legislative review of requests for new programs. This latter approach permits institutions to bring new projects and programs to the attention of the legislature without jeopardizing the basic funding base of the institution. Finally, a limited number of institutions, such as the University of Michigan, are constitutionally autonomous (not subject to regulation by other state agencies) and thus are treated in the legislative budget process as is any other state agency.

The role of state appropriations for private institution is much more narrow than within the public sector. State appropriations for private institutions are usually limited to specific programs that meet state priorities and interests. This might include support for medical education, teacher education, or programs that help students prepare to work with persons with disabilities. In addition, state support for private institutions may come in the form of capital budget support (see section to follow) or direct financial aid to students.

Tuition

Undergraduate tuition is the engine that drives much of higher education in the private sector and is becoming (as noted earlier) more important in the public sector. The states of Virginia and Vermont provide excellent examples of this trend. In those states, the flagship institutions do not rely on state appropriations as the main source of support for the operating budget.

The cost of tuition can be calculated on the basis of each credit hour taken or on a full-time enrollment basis. In this age of increased consumerism, many institutions are abandoning the practice of charging for each credit hour to avoid student and parental complaints such as "I spent X number of dollars on that course and did not learn anything, and I want a refund."

In private institutions, tuition is a critical component of the institutional budget (see Figure 1.2 on page 24). In smaller or struggling institutions, enrollment (and thus tuition dollars) can be the difference between meeting the revenue needed for the operating budget of the institution or failing to do so.

Public institutions often have statutory restrictions regarding the amount of tuition that may be charged to in-state residents. The rationale for such restrictions is that the state already allocates money to the institution and the citizens of the state should not have to pay an exorbitant amount in order to attend "their" state college or university. Usually there are no such restrictions on out-of-state tuition, and the institution or system may be free to charge with appropriate approvals whatever the traffic will bear. Artificial restrictions on the amount of in-state tuition that can be charged create unique fiscal challenges for state institutions, and many are seeking legislative relief in order to more adequately fund the enterprise.

Graduate tuition, whether it is paid by the student, from a grant, or through a tuition waiver program linked to an assistantship, does not begin to pay the cost for graduate education. Exceptions to this rule include specialized master's degree programs offered on a part-time basis for full-tuition paying students. Doctoral programs usually are costly to the institution and are only rarely offset by direct tuition payments or grant support. Professional school programs also provide similar budgetary challenges for the institution. Graduate programs are certainly essential in a research or comprehensive institution for their ability to attract top-flight faculty and students and their role in expanding knowledge. However, in a fiscal sense, they are not moneymakers or contributors to the funding stream for any institution.

Mandatory Student Fees

At public institutions and increasingly at private colleges and universities, student fees have been earmarked as one means to obtain revenue without raising tuition. In the highly politicized context for higher education, imposition of student fees is seen as a way to avoid confrontations on the issue of tuition. Such fees are usually charged on a term basis and are assessed from, at least, all undergraduate students. Examples include building use fees, technology fees, bond revenue fees, laboratory fees, breakage fees, recreation fees, student services fees, and student activity fees. Such fees are usually dedicated as support for a specific building or programs and must be reserved for those uses. To illustrate, a steady stream of income from a mandatory student fee is the fiscal foundation for selling bonds for many student recreation buildings.

The process of allocating mandatory student fees varies from institution to institution. In some institutions, mandatory fees are routinely allocated to support units as part of the general budget process. In others, a committee with student representation allocates the fees for use by departments and programs. In many cases, mandatory student activity fees are solely allocated by student government structures under the general supervision of some administrative agency.

Private institutions are much less likely to adopt the strategy of mandatory student fees as a means to generate income. Many of the programs and services at public institutions that are supported by such general student fees are funded from tuition income in private institutions. This is particularly true of programs and services that serve all students such as student centers and recreation programs. For private institutions the public relations fallout of adding general student fees to already high tuition bills is not worth the effort.

Special Student Fees

There are two types of special student fees that are used as a means of budget support: one-time fees and fees for services. Both types of special use student fees are present in both public and private institutions.

One-time fees are assessed for participation in a specific program or activity. Examples of one-time fees include study abroad fees, loan processing fees, and graduation fees. The income from the fee helps to offset the cost of the specific program without causing a drain on other institutional resources.

Fees for services are a growing phenomenon in higher education and are usually linked to psychological services, health care, or the ability of students to attend popular intercollegiate athletic events. To illustrate, in many counseling centers students seeking help are provided a limited number of sessions at no cost but must provide some form of co-payment to continue therapy or group sessions. There is great debate over whether fees should be charged for services, as often those who need the services most are least likely to be able to pay. While the debate continues, the fee-for-services approach to meeting revenue needs continues to expand. Athletic fees are also optional at some institutions and permit students to gain admission to popular athletic contests without charge or at a reduced charge.

Endowment Income

Income from the institutional endowment is a major source of support in private institutions. Overall fiduciary responsibility for managing the endowment rests with the institutional governing board, although day-by-day management issues are the responsibility of institutional staff. The income from the investment of the endowment is used to support the yearly operating budget of the institution. Endowment income can either be part of the central budget appropriation to the unit or in some cases departments or units have endowment funds directly designated to their unit.

Prudent institutions do not use all of the income generated by investing the endowment for current operations. Instead, rules are established, by the governing board, regarding the percentage of the endowment income that may be spent on operations for any fiscal year. Such spending limits create a more stable revenue stream for the institution, as it is not buffeted as much by the winds of change in the economy. Most important, spending limits aid in building the corpus of the endowment to assure funding for future generations of scholars and students.

How large should an endowment be in order to assure the fiscal health of the private institution? As each institution is unique, that question will depend on a number of factors, including the dependence of the institution on the endowment for annual operating funds. One measure of the strength of the endowment is the amount of money in the endowment for each full-time student.

Currently, most major public institutions have much more modest endowments than their private counterparts. That is likely to change in the future as state appropriated support for public higher education diminishes and alternative sources of revenue are needed. Whereas in private institutions the endowment is under the control of the governing board, that is not necessarily the case in public institutions. At some public institutions, independent foundations have been established to raise money and invest it for the good of the institution. Any foundation must meet the requirements of state statutes and regulations in the state where the foundation is located. The organization and control for such independent foundations will vary. For example, some have institutional representatives on their governing board, some do not. Some are absolutely independent, and some receive office space and clerical and accounting support from the institution. Each situation is unique and often is dependent on the history and tradition of the institution. If that is the case, the management challenges for the institutional chief executive are enormous, for the CEO does not control a critical source of funds to support the enterprise.

Many institutions, both public and private, have very limited endowment funds and some do not have any such support. When there is not substantial endowment support, the institution is in a state of constant uncertainty regarding the fiscal future, and planning and institutional growth are thwarted.

Fund-Raising

Identifying and obtaining private financial support from alumni, friends, parents, business, industry, and foundations is essential to the financial health of private institutions and is becoming increasingly important in public institutions. There are two types of fund-raising: annual giving and long-term campaigns for programs and projects.

Annual Giving

For most private institutions, annual giving is a critical revenue source for the operating budget of the institution. Revenue goals are set for the development of the institution based on past performance with increments added on for inflation. Donors designate some annual gifts for specific units or programs. Such gifts are usually not incremental to the unit but provide a welcome means of relief for the central budget of the institution. When a gift is not designated it becomes part of the general revenue stream for the institution. Establishment of a robust annual giving program is essential to the financial health of most private institutions of higher education.

Campaigns

To meet the needs for new facilities and programs many institutions conduct multiyear campaigns. In recent years such campaigns have evidenced a greater emphasis on program support as opposed to "bricks and mortar." Included in such initiatives are undergraduate scholarship programs, endowed chairs and professorships, and specific endowments to support specialized programs such as centers for the study of humanities.

Still other institutions raise funds for specific programs and needs as opposed to a comprehensive campaign. This precise form of fund-raising relies on in-depth knowledge of donor interests and compatibility of those interests with institutional needs.

Whatever the approach to fund-raising adopted by an institution, it is clear that fund-raising on both an annual and long-term basis is becoming more important at both public and private institutions. It is tempting to accept any and all gifts offered to the institution, but astute managers must examine whether the gift will be additive or will in the long run cost the institution more than the initial gift. There is an old adage in fund-raising: "beware of the gift that eats."

Finally, coordination of fund-raising activities is essential, for it is not in the best interests of the institution for potential donors to be approached by several institutional units at the same time. It is essential that someone be in charge of what requests are being made in the name of the institution and assure that small requests do not forgo potential larger donations.

Grants and Contracts

Research is supported in large part through grants from the federal government, state agencies, business and industry, and private foundations.

In addition to providing direct support in terms of salaries and operating costs of the specific research activity, grants also are required to recapture some of the indirect costs of the institution related to the grant. Indirect costs include, for example, services provided by the institution such as accounting and purchasing, as well as space renovation, maintenance and utilities, and administration. The federal government indirect cost rate is a set amount of the total grant request. It is negotiated between the federal government and the institution and applies to all federal research grants. Indirect costs are also assessed on grants from other sources, although those rates may be different from the rate established by the federal government. Charges for indirect costs do not accrue in the unit budget but are considered part of the general revenue stream in support of the institution.

Contracts are time-limited arrangements with business, industry, or government whereby the institution provides a direct service in return for payment. Examples of contracts include providing training for a state agency, teaching an academic course for the employees of a specific company, or providing technical computer support to another entity. Such contracts usually include an overhead line that covers some of the same items as does the indirect cost rate noted earlier. The institution establishes the overhead rate for all such contracts, and the money is returned for general use by the institution. Most institutions have centralized approval of proposals for grants and contracts. Such centralization assures that appropriate agreement by authorized institutional personnel has been given for any fiscal support of the proposal from the institution. In addition calculations for indirect costs and salaries and benefits can be checked for accuracy. If the proposal receives funding, the centralized grants and contracts office supervises fund disbursement and supervises any reporting requirements for the grant or contract. A first step in developing any proposal for a grant or contract is contact with the office in charge of such activities.

Auxiliary Services

Auxiliary services usually do not receive any institutional support and are expected to generate sufficient income to cover all operating expenses and long-term facility costs associated with the unit. Thus, they are deemed to be self-supporting. Although auxiliary services receive no institutional funds, they are governed by the same institutional rules regarding compensation, purchasing, and human resources. Each institution defines what programs and activities will be designated as auxiliary services. Examples of auxiliary services include student housing, food services, student unions, recreation programs, and, at times, intercollegiate athletics. Auxiliary enterprises must develop, as part of their budget strategies, fiscal support to maintain, renovate, and construct facilities. Long-term repair and renovation programs are generally funded through development of reserve funds either through transfers from the operating budget or deposit of excess income over expenses at the end of the fiscal year. Such reserve funds are dedicated for the specific purpose of facility construction, maintenance, or repair for the unit and usually cannot be used for other purposes.

In addition to meeting all expenses and long-term facility needs, an auxiliary enterprise is also expected to pay overhead to the institution to cover the costs of institutional services used by the auxiliary unit. This becomes part of the general revenue stream of the institution. Finally, if an auxiliary enterprise loses money through poor budget management or overly optimistic revenue-expense forecasting, the auxiliary is expected to cover the deficit from reserves or from the next year's operating budget.

Special Programs

Such programs may be one-time events such as a department-sponsored seminar or conference where entrance or registration fees are charged or recurring programs such as sports camps or continuing education seminars. In either case, the program must be self-supporting unless specific institutional permission has been given to have expenses exceed income. Revenue is usually retained by the unit to offset expenses. The goal of the enterprise is to break even at the end of the year. Modest reserve funds may be established for such units in order to handle situations where projected income falls short of the budget. If this happens on a continuing basis or if expenses routinely exceed the budget, review of the pricing policies involved in the program or institutional review of the efficacy of the program may be in order. Before any plans are made or implemented for a special program, appropriate approval for the venture must be received.

Contracted Institutional Services

In both public and private institutions, functions such as food service, bookstores, and custodial services are increasingly being outsourced to private enterprise. Through competitive bidding processes such contracts can become a source of funds to support both operations and capital expenditures such as facility repair, renovation, and new construction. Negotiation of those contracts may include yearly lump sum payments for capital expenses in addition to regular payments to the institution based on a percentage of gross sales.

The concept of contracted institutional services has been expanded on some campuses to include exclusive use contracts for soft drinks or other merchandise on campus. Under those contracts the entire institution adopts a certain brand of soft drink (or athletic equipment supplier, or vending machine operator, or telephone service, or food service management) and for that exclusive market the company makes lump sum payments each year to the institution in addition to a percentage of gross sales. Any contracts for institutional services should be reviewed by institutional legal counsel because the contract commits the institution to certain actions. In addition, the individual signing the contract on behalf of the institution must have clear authority to do so. Finally, supervision of the contract to assure vendor compliance must occur.

Church Support

Church-supported or church-related private institutions of higher education also rely on denominational financial support. Such support usually carries with it the requirement for representation on the governing board of the institution and assurances that the values of the religious group will be supported through institutional policies and programs. In many church-affiliated institutions, the amount of direct denominational support as a proportion of the institutional budget has diminished in recent years.

State Capital Budgets

In some states, capital development funds for new facilities or facility renovation at public institutions are handled through a separate funding process. Capital support for facilities can be requested through a process that is in addition to the regular appropriation process. Usually those funds are limited, and only facilities that meet the highest priorities of the state higher education coordinating board are funded. At times, private institutions may also be able to access state capital funds if the facility or the program meets a pressing state need.

Federal Capital Support

If a new building is consistent with a federal need and if there is support for the building in the federal appropriations process, then federal dollars may also be available to institutions for capital construction projects. These appropriations are very important for construction of complicated and expensive research and medical facilities.

Other Sources of Income

There are a number of miscellaneous sources of income used to support programs and facilities within higher education. Facility rental fees, particularly for large concert halls and performance venues, help offset operational costs for those facilities. The privilege of parking requires parking permits that all eligible community members (including faculty, staff, and students) must purchase. Rental fees for specialized pieces of equipment such as stadium field coverings are but one example of the creative ways unit budget managers generate income in support of their program. Although individually such sources of support seem to be small in relationship to the institutional budget, in the aggregate such income sources are critical to the financial health of the institution's various units.

PUBLIC VERSUS PRIVATE FINANCIAL ISSUES

Whereas in the past the funding for higher education differed markedly between public and private institutions, those differences are becoming increasingly blurred. Figure 1.2 compares and contrasts the sources of funds for all public and all private not-for–profit institutions across the country.

Note that the percentage assigned to the various sources of revenue will vary considerably between institutions of the same type. Well-endowed institutions, for example, have a much larger part of their operating budget covered by interest income from the endowment. As demands for the use of state funds continue to grow, public institutions have adopted many of the strategies of private institutions in obtaining funds to support educational endeavors. Both public and private institutions are seeking outside funding to support institutional goals in ever greater amounts. What differs is the degree of control on matters of finance that is exercised beyond the campus.

Exhibit 1.2. Questions to Consider Regarding Sources of Support for Your Unit.

1. What sources of funds support the operations of your budget unit?
2. Does any of the financial support for your unit come from mandatory student fees? If so:
   a. Are there restrictions on the use of the money?
   b. Does the process of requesting funds differ from the regular institutional budget process? In what ways?
   c. What approvals are necessary to reallocate student fee money if it has already been approved for another purpose?
3. Is the budget for your unit supported by any special student fees or fees for services? If so, how are these fees determined?
4. What responsibility and opportunities, if any, exist for fund-raising by your unit?
5. Are there grants or contracts being administered through your unit? If so, what responsibilities do you have for fiscal management of the grant or contract?
6. If your unit is an auxiliary enterprise, what long-term plans are in place for the repair and renovation of physical facilities? How will they be funded?
7. Is your unit sponsoring any special programs in this fiscal year? What are the financial expectations for such ventures?
8. Are you as a budget manager, providing oversight for any contracted institutional services? If so, what are your responsibilities under the contract?

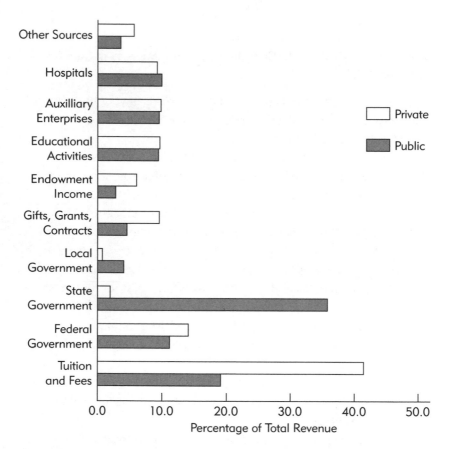

Figure 1.2. Percentage Comparison of Sources of Income for All Public and Private Institutions in the United States.[1]

Adapted from the data of the National Center for Educational Statistics (1997) [http://www.nces.ed.gov]

    1. Total revenues do not sum to 100 percent due to rounding.

Control and Approvals

In private institutions, financial policies, investment strategies and institutional policies are controlled either through the governing board or through other campus-based governance and administrative bodies. This approach provides greater degrees of freedom in using resources to meet unexpected needs or problems. For example, in the last two decades, meeting the rising cost of energy required reallocation at many private institutions, but permission for that reallocation did not have to be sought beyond the campus. For public institutions often permission must be sought from the system, the state coordinating board or other oversight body, or the legislature itself to change the uses of legislative appropriations.

Policies

Fiscal policies at private institutions are likely to be less cumbersome, permitting transfers of funds for reasonable purposes without many approvals and other bureaucratic barriers. The budget manager is, however, held accountable for making sure that at the end of the fiscal year there is no deficit.

In public institutions, usually the institutional budget office must grant permission for line item transfers over a certain dollar amount. Sometimes for certain categories of expenditures the governing board or the supervising state higher education agency must approve such transfers.

Human Resource Issues

In both types of institutions, there is concern for growth in the number of positions in the institution. Adding new positions in public universities is usually more difficult than in the private sector, although in both arenas the budget manager must account for both direct and indirect costs associated with such positions, and the funds must be available to pay for them.

Compensation for faculty and staff are major issues in both public and private institutions. The growth of technology in particular has made persons with technical backgrounds highly sought after in the marketplace. Higher education, in both sectors, has had to develop new compensation guidelines to keep and attract technical staff, and traditional compensation models simply do not work. The issue of adequate compensation for technical and support staff is one that is common to both public and private institutions.

Unions are present at both public and private institutions and create special human resource issues, including work rules and compensation. A union environment creates a special case for handling issues of employee discipline, work loads, and reward structures.

Both types of institutions also must comply with state and federal regulations and laws relating to issues of equal opportunity, disabilities, sexual harassment, worker's compensation, civil rights, and health and safety. Budget managers must be aware of the legal, budgetary, and institutional requirements regarding personnel matters. For example, the institution usually has pay scales for certain types of positions, and those scales cannot be ignored in making new hires.

Purchasing

Public and private institutions have regulations regarding purchasing goods and services. For many public institutions, purchasing of goods and services is complicated by state regulations and required state contracts for certain items. When a state contract is in place for a certain product, then a manager must show cause to not purchase from that source. State blanket contracts add a degree of complexity to any purchase. State institutions may also be subject to requirements that the lowest bidder gets the contract if they meet the minimum requirements for the service or goods. Such requirements can cause a number of difficulties for the academic manager.

Usually at private institutions, purchasing requirements are less rigid and are not complicated by state contracts. In fact, purchasing for some items may be highly decentralized in a private institution, with the unit taking responsibility for seeking bids and making the decision on a contract. Whereas on the surface such freedom can be very attractive, it also requires that each academic manager exercise due diligence in managing the resources of the institution under their control.(See Chapter Four for further discussion on the pitfalls of financial management.)

Audit Requirements

Audit requirements exist in both private and public institutions. An external audit provides an independent review of the decisions made by fiscal managers. Both financial and management reports are issued, and the budget manager and other administrative officials review the reports and agree to needed changes in unit policies and procedures to comply with the audit findings. A regular follow-up is then conducted to make sure the recommended changes have been made.

In some institutions, there is an internal audit office that regularly conducts audits of all departments of the institution. If a manager is lucky enough to be in such an institution, use of the internal audit office can strengthen budgetary and procedural oversight within the unit. As a new manager, it is a good practice to ask the internal audit office to conduct an audit of the unit to identify problems or weaknesses in financial and budgetary procedures.

In other institutions, audits are scheduled and performed by an outside firm. Public institutions have the added complication of audits from the state level. A negative audit finding by the state agency can be a source of both institutional embarrassment and problems.

WHY DOES ALL THIS MATTER?

Understanding the sources of funds for support of institutional programs and services is a first step in developing a sound fiscal strategy as a manager. Each source of funds provides unique opportunities and constraints on the budget manager. Understanding the strength and limitations of fund sources helps the manager plan more effectively and make more realistic budget requests. For example, if student fee income is legally dedicated only to the construction and maintenance of a specific building, then it is naïve to ask for some of that income to be diverted to ongoing operations.

In addition, the budget requests for one unit may have implications for another. To illustrate, the budget manager of the learning disabilities clinic on campus sees a quick solution to the need for more money to operate the clinic: charge students for the screening tests that up to this time were offered without charge. This approach to solving a budget dilemma has ramifications far beyond the clinic. A fee-for-services approach might, for example, influence the financial aid budget or the athletic budget, or it might have legal implications for the institution. When it comes to money, unilateral decisions cannot be made by any part of the institution without unexpected ramifications.

It is true that many similarities exist between the fiscal realities faced by private and public institutions; there are also differences in the development of policies and programs. Understanding those differences and the unique policies of your institutional type will help you as budget manager be more effective. For example, in most public institutions it is important to control the number of positions within the institution. Unbridled growth of the workforce is neither desired nor permitted. If you are in such an institution, then your budget request for support of a new position will need detailed justification even if you have the resources within your budget. You may have the money but may not have the authority to create a new position line. If, however, a well-endowed private institution may pay more attention to control of the bottom line than the addition of positions, then your rationale for the new position must be couched in terms of how the unit will stay within the approved budget even with the addition of a position. There are many more such examples. The essential point is that budget managers understand the important funding priorities and the procedures to support them in their institution.

Astute budget managers understand the sources of funds supporting the institution, their units, and the limitations on use of those funds. Such knowledge aids budget managers in developing realistic budgets and requests for additional budget support.

REFERENCE

Schuh, J. "Fiscal Pressures on Higher Education and Student Affairs." In M. J. Barr and Mary K. Desler (eds.), *The Handbook of Student Affairs Administration*. San Francisco: Jossey-Bass, 2000.

2

Unraveling the Budget

BUDGETS IN HIGHER EDUCATION are very simple if they are examined from the perspective of Mayhew (1979), who stated that "budgets are really a statement of educational purpose phrased in fiscal terms" (p. 54). Sometimes as a manager it is difficult to keep that definition in mind as you confront budget cycles, budget rules, and budget complexity. Unraveling the budget is often like pulling on a skein of yarn—information, policies, and procedures are sometimes so intertwined that they are difficult to separate and understand. In this volume the term *budget* is applied to the entire institutional budget as well as to the specific budget of an individual department or program unit. The discussion in this chapter will focus on institutional budgets, but the purposes for budgets and the models for developing budgets are equally applicable to individual program and unit budgets.

This chapter is designed to increase understanding of the terms involved in budgeting and the implications the budget has for your work as an academic fiscal manager. The chapter begins with a discussion of purposes of budgets, the types of budgets involved in higher education, and the various kinds of budgeting models that may be employed in an institution of higher education. Next, the key elements of the budget are examined. Finally, decision-making processes on fiscal matters are also examined. Understanding the types of budgets at the institution and the general budget model used by the institution to develop budget guidelines and the processes of decision making will assist you in becoming a better academic financial manager.

THE PURPOSES OF A BUDGET

Why do institutions put so much time and energy into developing and implementing a budget plan? There are many purposes for a budget. Maddox (1999) defines five general purposes for a budget: putting business strategy into operation, allocating resources, providing incentives, giving control, and providing a means of communication both within and without the organization.

Putting Business Strategy into Operation

Like any business, income comes into the institution, and invoices for goods and services must be paid. Higher education is usually a not-for-profit enterprise (the exception being proprietary schools). Any excess income over expenses at the end of a fiscal year is used to help finance the future of the enterprise, meet pressing operating costs, construction, or infrastructure needs, or in some public institutions reverts to the state. In contrast to business and industry, profits are not part of the lexicon of higher education.

The institutional budget reflects the plans, priorities, goals, and aspirations that drive the institution. The budget is a blueprint of what is important. For example, if the institution has adopted a goal of having the best business school in the country, then the budget will reflect support for that unit. Or if the institution is committed to keeping access open to low-income students, the student financial aid budget will rise in direct proportion to adopted increases in tuition, fees, and room and board charges. Finally, if the institution has established a goal of retaining faculty and support staff, then the budget will reflect increased compensation and benefit dollars. Each institution has unique and sometimes conflicting priorities and goals, and the astute budget manager understands those goals as requests are made for financial support.

Sometimes the budget is not goal directed but instead is focused on identifying resources to cover costs, such as utilities. The institution does not have a strategic goal of paying higher utility costs, but must do so in order to provide basic educational services. In other words, some priorities of an institution simply involve keeping the doors open.

Careful examination of the budget of the unit and of the institution can help academic managers understand both the problems and the priorities of the institution. This understanding, in turn, helps managers become more adept in garnering resources for the programs and priorities of their unit and spending them wisely.

Allocating Resources

The reality is that no institution of higher education has unlimited resources and the ability to meet all the needs and wants of all constituencies and units. For purposes of both financial management and understanding, decision makers must make a clear distinction between needs and wants. On the one hand, a *need* is an essential element of the service, program, or instructional unit that must be funded in order to meet institutional expectations. For example, if English is required for all entering freshman and the freshman class is larger than expected, then the English Department may need additional instructors. Note that the word *may* has been deliberately used in this example. Strong budget management requires more than just allocating more money to support additional instructors in English. Other alternatives should be carefully explored before making such a budget adjustment. Examples of alternatives scenarios include modestly increasing the size of each section of freshman English or rescheduling some sections into peak demand times for students; if an analysis reveals that such changes still will not provide instruction for all entering students, then the institution is faced with two choices: adjust the budget to increase the resources to the unit or modify the requirement regarding freshman English. Either decision has consequences (intended and unintended) that must be understood by decision makers.

A *want,* on the other hand, is something desired by the unit or an individual member of the unit. A want may have the potential to move both the unit and the institution forward, but it is not essential to either the operation of the unit or the institution. To illustrate, an academic unit might have a goal of equipping all classrooms that they use with state-of-the-art technology. Although "smart classrooms" might enhance student learning, instruction is already offered in those facilities without such additional cost. Another way to address this want would be to develop a multiyear plan to retrofit all classrooms. At times, wants are simply amenities that would make life easier but are not essential to either the institution or the unit. State-of-the-art gadgets often fall into this category of wants.

The budget reflects the varying sources of funds that support the mission of the institution. If a unit has a special endowment or has the ability to generate income through contracts and grants, fewer institutional funds may be allocated to that unit. An effective institutional budget assures that the general funds of the institution are used to support the highest priorities and the greatest needs of the entire institution.

Providing Incentives

A budget should also provide incentives for sound management of fiscal resources. Sometimes the institutional rules governing budgets are structured in ways that work against sound fiscal management. For example, on many campuses at the end of the fiscal year there is a frenzy of spending. Supplies are ordered in bulk, computers are purchased, and so forth. This activity is usually caused by budget rules that require excess funds in a unit budget to revert back to the control of the central administration or the state. Sometimes the purchases that are made at the end of the fiscal year are needed, but often they are unnecessary. If that is the case, precious fiscal resources are then wasted. A better approach to budgeting is to provide an incentive for managers to keep a tight rein on expenses. One method is to allow the unit to retain some, if not all, of the money left in the budget at the end of the fiscal year. This money could then be placed in a reserve account to support major purchases for the unit or facility renovation, or carried forward to be used in the next budget year for other expenses. Such strategies actually save money for the institution and help conserve resources.

Giving Control

Maddox (1999) asserts that the most traditional role of the budget is to exert fiscal control within the institution. There are two philosophies regarding budget control within higher education: highly centralized budgetary decisions and unit-centered budget decisions. Under the highly centralized model, a central budgeting authority reviews all expenditures that exceed X number of dollars. The theory behind such centralized control is to assure that the funds allocated to the unit are being used for the purposes that were intended. It is both a costly and time-consuming method of assuring sound fiscal management.

Under a decentralized model, each unit budget manager is held responsible for assuring that expenditures are being made in a prudent and effective manner. This approach requires that academic budget managers be trained in fiscal management and also understand the rules and regulations for fiscal matters within the institution. It also requires that managers seek help when they are faced with a problem. If the goals and objectives of the institution are clearly understood by all budget managers and if unit budget managers are held accountable for their actions and decisions, then decentralized budget control can be quite effective.

Most institutions have developed a hybrid of the centralized and decentralized model. Most routine decisions are left to the academic budget manager; central budget control is exercised over large fund expenditures. Under such a system, intervention will occur only if problems such as deficit spending are identified within the unit budget. This combination approach seems to work quite well, providing some measure of institutional control yet allowing greater degrees of freedom for those who are closest to problems and issues within the unit.

Providing Means of Communication

As Mayhew (1979) indicated, the budget is a tool for communication to a variety of publics. Decisions regarding where resources are allocated and what are the priorities within the institution are immediately understood by review of the budget and the budget guidelines. For example, if retention of faculty is an important institutional goal, then the merit increment pool for faculty may be larger than that for other members of the institutional workforce. Or if installation and maintenance of a new computer network is a top priority, then the allocation to the technology unit will reflect the cost of those efforts.

In public institutions, the institutional budget also provides a means to communicate to key constituency groups what is important to the institution. These groups include the legislature and the state board of higher education as well as other constituency groups. In many states, the institutional budget is a public document and can be reviewed by anyone, including the student press. This makes for interesting debates over what is important and what is not important within the institution.

Private institutions are more apt to consider budget documents as private information. No requirement exists for private institutions to share this information. Both types of institutions must make budget documents available for review by funders, including foundations, private donors, and the state and federal government. The institutional budget shows funding entities what the institution intends to do with the money they are requesting and how this request aligns with other institutional priorities.

Finally, the budget is the primary means for the institutional administration to convey to the governing board the real priorities of the institution. Although planning processes and program reviews provide interesting materials for board review, it is the budget that specifically informs the governing board where institutional resources are being spent and that, in turn, highlights the priorities of the academic and administrative management team.

The fiduciary responsibility of the governing board requires careful review of the budget to assure that sound fiscal management policies are in place. If, for example, the fund-raising goal for the institution is doubled in one year as a strategy to balance the budget, then the governing board should question whether that is a realistic or prudent goal. At some institutions, the budget review is conducted and debated by the full governing board. Most often, however, the executive and finance committees of the governing board review the budget in detail and their reports are presented for board action.

Summary

It is clear that the budget is more than a set of numbers. An institutional budget is a fluid document that reflects the goals and priorities of the institution and has the flexibility to respond to changing needs and problems. The budget reflects strategy, provides control and communication, should encourage sound management, and is the means to allocate the limited resources of the institution.

TYPES OF BUDGETS

Each institution has unique budgeting guidelines and budget processes. However, in general there are three major types of budgets on any campus: the operating budget, the capital budget, and auxiliary budgets. There also may be separate function budgets for specialized units such as research operations or hospitals. For purposes of this chapter, discussion will be limited to operating budgets and capital budgets. Auxiliary budgets (see Chapter One) are governed by the same institutional requirements and differ from the operating budget and the capital budget only in the source of funds and the self-supporting nature of the enterprise.

Operating Budget

The operating budget is the core budget for the institution and is based on a fiscal year (Woodard and von Destinon, 2000). According to Meisinger and Dubeck (1984), an operating budget reflects all income from all sources, including restricted funds as well as all approved expenditures for the fiscal year (pp. 7–8). In addition, some institutions keep a separate cash budget to monitor the influx of revenue and the use made of those monies. At most institutions, the cash budget is subsumed as a part of the general operating budget of the institution.

The institutional operating budget is shaped by institutional rules and fiscal policies. For example, the largest line item in any operating budget in higher education involves personnel, including faculty and professional and support staff. Usually decisions are made at an institutional level regarding the amount of money available to increase the number of faculty and staff, faculty and staff salary increments, and compensation for promotion decisions. Even if a unit has sufficient resources, the unit is not permitted to spend more money than is approved through these central guidelines. Thus, the institutional priority of increasing positions, titles, rank, or compensation reflected in the operating budget is centrally controlled.

The fiscal year will vary from institution to institution and is governed by the academic calendar. Some fiscal years run from September 1 through August 31, allowing for all costs of summer operations to be included in the same fiscal year. Others begin July 1 and run through June 30, primarily due to the start date of the fall semester prior to September 1 or to the state fiscal year. Rarely do institutions of higher education have a fiscal year that begins on January 1 and ends on December 31, as is often true in business and industry. In any case, it is extremely important to understand the actual dates for the fiscal year in your institution as it will help in fiscal management. The "bottom line" at the end of the fiscal year will demonstrate whether the organization is operating in the red or the black.

Finally, the operating budget reflects the amount of money that is approved for various expenditures to operate all of the units within the institution. The fiscal rules involving moving money from one line item to another will vary by institution and by the public or private nature of the enterprise. Whatever the type of institution, however, academic managers are expected to control costs and close the fiscal year in the black. If there is a problem in meeting the goal of budget expectations, then the manager must seek help from the central budget office or other administrative staff.

Capital Budgets

Capital budgets reflect the money set aside to improve the physical plant of the institution and to finance new construction, major pieces of equipment, replacement of vehicles, or expenses such as those associated with technology that are investments for the institution beyond the current operating year. It should be noted that all capital expenses are not necessarily budgeted in the capital budget. Desktop computers, for example, have value beyond the current operating year, but replacement costs are often funded as part of the operating budget of the institution. In general, the capital budget is reserved for large projects that may take several years to complete and that have an impact beyond the current year of operation. Repair and renovation funds for classrooms, for example, fall into the category of capital expenses. Budget managers should understand the definition of capital expenses used at their institution.

The sources of funds for the capital budget are outlined in Chapter One. In most institutions, auxiliary enterprises are not able to access capital funds because such units are expected to generate sufficient income to cover repair, renovation, and new construction on their own. Sometimes public institutions have access to money through a capital budget fund that is allocated through the higher education coordinating board of the state. This capital budget funding is distinct from other sources of support for public institutions. At other institutions, capital development funds are earmarked as a special category of expense paid from the investment income of the endowment.

None of these sources of funds is usually sufficient to meet the total capital requirements of any college or university. So institutions of higher education, like municipalities, sell bonds to potential investors to make up the difference. In simple terms, the institution goes into debt to secure needed facilities or equipment. The total repayment cost for the capital projects funded through the sale of the bonds must also include the interest on that debt. The sale of and the financing structure for bonds is a complex process and will not be discussed in detail in this volume. As an academic budget manager, however, you need to know whether you are responsible for debt repayment including interest for any facilities under your jurisdiction. Usually such debt repayments are reflected as part of the operating budget, although the approval process for the construction and financing of the facility is part of the capital budgeting process. Note that the fiscal health of the institution is reflected in its bond rating.

BUDGET MODELS

There is more than one correct way to develop a budget, although some managers would have you believe otherwise. This section will discuss the various models used by colleges and universities in developing the budget and highlight the implications each model will have for your role as an academic manager.

Incremental Budgets

An incremental approach to budgeting is based on the assumption that both needs and costs vary only a small amount from year to year. It also assumes that the budget from the previous fiscal year is accurate and fairly reflects the expenditures of the unit. Both of these assumptions may be false. Nevertheless, most budgets in higher education are incremental. The budget from the current year becomes the base budget for purposes of calculating the amount of money required for a percentage increment to units.

Under the incremental budget model, all units in the institution receive the same percentage increases for the same line items within their budget. Those increases are based on the amount of money available and often use some index for inflation such as the *Higher Education Price Index* (Research Associates of Washington, 2002). There is no strategic examination of the expenditure patterns of the total institution or individual budget units. In addition, neither cost increases-decreases nor any increase-decrease in the numbers of students served or other increases-decreases in demand for services provided are examined.

To illustrate, a typical incremental budget may allocate money to units as follows: a 3 percent increase for salaries and benefits except for student workers, a 2 percent increase for telephone, a 5 percent increase for office supplies, a 1 percent increase for all other line items, and a 0 percent increase for travel. To prepare the budget, the academic manager only needs to adjust the base budget from the current year based on these percentages. Such incremental budget approaches are extremely easy to implement. Incremental budget increases also do not reflect the actual expenditures of the unit in the preceding fiscal year. In fact, if the initial budget of the unit does not accurately reflect program expenditures, then budget problems and inequities will only be compounded over many years of incremental budgeting.

Incremental budgeting models minimize conflict within the organization because every unit is treated in the same way. Incremental budgeting also avoids reexamination of current and past commitments in order to determine whether they still meet the needs of the institution. Maddox (1999) captures the frustration of incremental budgeting when he states: "However, incremental budgeting has no mechanism for making significant adjustments to allocation between units. A unit that has a generous budget will only get better off relative to other units—its 'extra' budget grows on that budget excess, whereas another unit treads water as essential funding is increased just (or not) enough to keep pace with cost increases" (p. 16).

Redistribution

At times institutions will combine incremental budgets with a redistribution process. This approach provides a general budget increase for operations but allows the budget manager to redistribute the dollars within all line items in the budget. The new budget cannot, however, be increased more than the allocation provided through the budget increment. Although slightly more complex to administer, a redistributed budget model allows managers to adjust line items to more accurately reflect the actual cost patterns of the unit. Redistribution within units still does not address, however, the inequities that occur between units.

Another version of a redistributed model is to provide the increment on the combined budgets of all units within an administrative organization such as a school, college, or division level. The dean or vice president can then address within-school or division inequities between units regarding items such as travel or supplies that have developed as a result of incremental budgeting. Allowing the redistributed model to occur at a higher level within the administrative organization is more cumbersome but has the advantages of partially addressing institutionwide inequities.

Zero-Based Budgets

The zero-based budget model requires that each item in the budget be justified and that nothing is assumed to always be a part of the budget process. Incremental funds are not automatically distributed in the institution, and every budget manager must justify every expense in his or her budget request. A zero-based budgeting model has the advantage of enabling careful review of all institutional expenditures and requires that all expenditures be linked to the strategic goals of the unit and the institution. Although zero-based budgeting identifies potential areas of cost savings for redistribution to other units, or central budget reserves, the process is time consuming, labor intensive, and frustrating. Because of the intense review required in a zero-based budgeting model, some institutions have modified the model to target certain aspects of the institutional budget or a certain proportion of the potential funds available for distribution within the institution. For example, an institution may decide to provide incremental funding for all expenditures except travel and apply the zero-based model to requests for travel funds. Or the institution may distribute most of the available resources on an incremental basis but require zero-based budget justifications to gain access to the funds that are held back centrally. Or a modified zero-based budget may be used wherein 90 percent of the unit budget is assumed and 10 percent must be completely justified.

Zero-based budgeting has great strength but only if it is firmly linked to strategic planning activities within the institution. If the process is working correctly, then funding is given to those programs and activities that are critical to the long-term success of the institution. Because it is time consuming some organizations opt to use the zero-based budgeting model only every five to ten years. Under such an approach an institution can reap the advantage of an objective review of both revenues and expenditures of the institution without yearly time-investment in zero-based budget development.

Planning, Programming, and Budgeting Systems Models (PPBS)

In the 1980s and early 1990s, the PPBS model was in favor in many institutions of higher education. It is based on an intensive planning process that defines all activities within the unit and provides an analysis of the cost effectiveness of those activities. The purpose of the analysis is to determine whether there is a more cost effective way to meet the same objective. PPBS, in practice, is both time and labor intensive, but it does link fiscal decisions directly to the planning processes and program-implementation processes of the institution. Effective PPBS systems rely on agreed upon goals and objectives for the institution and the unit, and achievement of goals is directly related to funding.

A major shortfall of the PPBS approach to budgeting is finding methods to adequately measure outcomes. This is particularly true in higher education, where a number of factors contribute to the education of a student and one cannot merely count the number of "widgets" produced within a certain period. PPBS is a budgeting system that makes sense in theory but is very difficult to implement and manage within higher education settings.

Formula Budgeting

Formula budgeting is the budget model used by most states to allocate money to state-supported institutions of higher education. Under a formula budgeting model, a mathematical ratio is developed that links each full-time student to a dollar figure. In other words a student taking fifteen hours is worth X number of dollars. In recent years, formula budgeting on the part of the state has become more sophisticated; funding formulas have been developed for full-time enrollment of graduate students, full-time enrollment of undergraduate students, and even for differences in upper-division or lower-division students as well as certain content areas such as medical education. Formula budgeting is designed to bring more objectivity and equity into the state funding process for public higher education, but because politically motivated special appropriations often exist most of that objectivity is diminished.

Formula funding has also been employed in institutional budgeting, but when used it exhibits many of the weaknesses that are displayed when it is applied at the state level. A formula based budget is centered on past behavior and does not account for changes in enrollment or needs in the next funding year. Therefore, formula funding rewards the status quo and does not provide incentives for sound management or innovation.

Cost or Responsibility Centered Management

Though slightly different, these two alternative budget strategies are grouped together for purposes of this discussion. Under a strict cost centered approach, each part of the organization is responsible for generating revenue to meet expenses and is expected to "stand on its own bottom." Although this works well for auxiliary enterprises, the model does not adapt itself easily to instructional and support units within the college or university.

Responsibility centered budgeting has been adopted in many institutions as a means to extend decision making for budget matters beyond the central administration (Woodward and von Destinon, 2000). Under a responsibility centered model, each unit is financially responsible for activities and is held accountable for expenditures. In the responsibility centered model, if a unit incurs a deficit because of unexpected circumstances or poor management, that deficit must be made up in the following fiscal year from allocated budget resources. If, on the other hand, the unit has excess income over expenditures, the unit is permitted to carry forward the surplus for reallocation or support of more important projects. Responsibility centered budgeting provides incentives and greater flexibility to meet changing priorities (Stocum and Rooney, 1997). It has the disadvantage of encouraging competition between units and concentrating on unit goals to the exclusion of institutional goals and objectives.

Summary

Most institutions do not use a pure form of any of these budget models. Instead adaptations are made in budgeting that fit the unique circumstances of the institution and the needs and priorities within the organization. Though the models for budgeting are important to understand, the processes whereby the budget is created are even more crucial to fiscal understanding.

BUDGET ELEMENTS

Simply stated, the two major elements in any budget are revenue and expenses. The key to successful budgeting is to be able to closely predict the revenue and assure that expenses do not exceed available funds. There is never any guarantee that the budget will accurately reflect what actually occurs in a given fiscal year, for as many have said, budgeting is an art rather than a science.

Revenue

The first step in budgeting is to identify all sources of funds that support the enterprise. For most academic managers the major source of funds comes through the institution in the form of an allocation. But in addition to allocated funds, departments may also have other sources of income (see Chapter One). Each revenue source should be examined to determine whether it is ongoing and stable, a one-time source, a discrete fund source, or a source that is subject to variability because it is dependent on the return from investments. Ongoing and stable sources of funds are usually those related to institutional funding of the program or service. One-time fund sources might be, for example, registration fees for a departmentally sponsored conference or symposium. Discrete fund sources are those that relate to outside funding for a specialized program or piece of equipment such as a grant to purchase a painting or a new electronic microscope. Those discrete sources of revenue cannot be spent on any other item and some-times cannot be spent in another fiscal year. Finally, variable income often relates to endowment funds that are invested in the market but are ear-marked for support of the department or program. The return on the in-vestment will change from year to year and is not predictable. Revenue from one-time sources, discrete fund sources, or variable sources should be predicted as conservative estimates, since there are no guarantees that op-timum conditions will prevail and the money will be available to cover all the expenses. Once all revenues are compiled and classified, it is clear what amount of money is anticipated to cover expenses.

Expenses

The best way to predict expenses is to approach the task from the zero-based budgeting model described earlier in this chapter. Through such a process the manager can identify the actual costs for a particular activity, such as a mailing to all new doctoral students entering the department. Some expenses are driven by factors beyond the control of the depart-ment, such as those related to inflation, centrally mandated personnel poli-cies, or goods and services contracts. Other expenses are driven by the increase or decrease of activity in the department. For example, if an ad-missions office has an increase of 5,000 applications, then the expense budget used to support processing applications will have to increase.

Most expense budgets segregate salaries and benefits from other items in the expense budget. Personnel is clearly the largest line item in higher education. Budgeting personnel costs relates to a variety of factors, includ-ing addition of positions, loss of positions, the need for temporary or sea-sonal workers, student employment practices, salary increases, changes in benefits, and outsourcing of certain personnel functions that were for-merly handled within the institution. It should be noted that personnel ex-pense items in the budget are segregated from other expenses, and special permission usually must be received to transfer money from the person-nel budget to cover other expenses within the department or vice versa. Or sometimes savings from staff turnover are captured on an institutional level and pooled so that the department does not have those dollars to re-allocate during the current fiscal year.

Required or Fixed Costs

Maddox (1999) defines required or fixed costs as those necessary to stay in business. Such expenses include office supplies, computer supplies, telephone service (including long distance), printing, computer supplies, monthly data connection fees, and so forth. In most academic departments, costs for utilities and facility maintenance are budgeted at the institutional level, but in some athletic and student service areas (particularly auxiliaries) those costs are allocated as part of the unit operating budget. Even though such costs are required, they should be examined to assure that there is not a more cost effective way to meet the departmental need.

Discretionary Costs

There are a number of discretionary costs in any departmental or program budget. Each should be examined to assure that it is necessary or whether less expensive alternatives can be identified. Examples of discretionary costs include travel, registration fees, program development, faculty and staff development, publicity and program promotion, honoraria, subscriptions, and so forth.

Some discretionary costs should be directly related to revenues. For example, if the Women's Center has decided to sell T-shirts at the annual "Take Your Daughters to Work" program on campus, the cost for purchasing and printing the T-shirts should be offset by revenue from such sales. Conservative estimates are needed in such cases for both expenses and revenue.

APPROACHES TO DECISION MAKING

Fundamentally there are two approaches to developing budgets: centralized or unit-based. Both have strengths and weaknesses. Rarely does an institution adopt a pure form of either approach.

Centralized

Under the centralized model, all decisions regarding the parameters of the budget are made at an institutional level. Strong controls are exercised to assure that budget expenditures are congruent with approved items and that units are following institutional budget rules. The broader institutional goals and realities drive the budget process. A centralized approach to budgeting serves many institutions very well. An institution that is in financial difficulty may adopt a centralized model in order to control costs and monitor certain expenditures. Under a centralized approach to decision making, it is much easier to make adjustments for unexpected cost variations and to capture savings for other pressing needs. Centralization easily permits redistribution of scarce dollars without a great deal of debate and gnashing of teeth.

A highly centralized approach to budgeting does not, however, encourage sound management within units. There are few if any incentives for a unit to employ cost-saving measures because there is little reward for doing so. Morale regarding matters of finance is usually lower under a centralized budget approach, since managers feel they have little or no input into decisions that influence their programs and activities. Finally, a great deal of time and energy is expended in finding methods to get around the system and manipulate resources.

Unit-Based

A unit-based approach to budgeting reverses the information flow in developing the budget. It is based on the premise that those closest to operations have a more complete understanding of the real financial needs of the unit. Instead of information flowing from the top of the organization to the units, each unit generates a budget request that reflects the needs of that unit. The unit-based approach to budgeting is more complicated and time consuming but does increase the involvement level of academic managers and the sense that their needs are being considered in the budget process.

Unit-based budgeting approaches have two weaknesses. First, such approaches encourage a myopic view of fiscal matters. The driving force is the unit rather than addressing larger institutional issues. Such a focus discourages cooperation and increases competition between units. Second, it may encourage unrealistic expectations. Unless there is feedback prior to the beginning of the budget process on the realistic limitations facing the institution, unit managers tend to increase their expectations of what is possible. When those expectations are not met, managers and faculty and staff become discouraged and feel their input is not important.

Combination

Most institutions have developed a hybrid approach to budget development. Information is shared with unit managers prior to budget submission regarding the opportunities and the limitations facing the institution in the coming year. Some general guidelines are set with regard to expense items such as increments to compensation, including benefits. In addition, general guidelines are also communicated regarding indirect cost rates for research or auxiliary enterprises.

Unit budget managers then develop their budget requests based on information, not wishful thinking. Within those broad guidelines, they are able to submit both revenue and expense requests that more closely reflect the needs of their unit whether it is an academic department or a support service. Although the unit may not always receive everything that is requested, greater understanding is achieved regarding the reasons for eventual budget decisions. A shared approach increases the ability of faculty and staff involved in the budget process to understand what factors influence decisions. (See Exhibit 2.1.)

CONCLUSION

Budgeting in higher education is not a simple task. Academic managers are faced with both controllable and uncontrollable costs, as well as limitations on the resources available to them. In order to be successful in such an environment, it is critical that the academic manager understand the many purposes of the budget and the general models of budget development. Such a base of understanding helps budget managers determine what information to gather and how to present requests for resources more effectively.

REFERENCES

Maddox, D. C. *Budgeting for Not-for-Profit Organizations.* New York: Wiley, 1999.

Mayhew, L. B. *Surviving the Eighties: Strategies and Procedures for Solving Fiscal and Enrollment Problems.* San Francisco: Jossey-Bass, 1979.

Meisinger, R. J., and Dubeck, L. W. *College and University Budgeting: An Introduction for Faculty and Academic Administrators*. Washington, D.C.: National Association of College and University Business Officers, 1984.

Research Associates of Washington. *Higher Education Price Index (HEPI)*. Washington D.C.: Research Associates of Washington, 2002.

Stocum, D. L., and Rooney, P. M. "Responding to Resource Constraints: A Departmentally Based System of Responsibility Centered Management." *Change,* 1997, *29*(5), 51–67.

Woodard, D. B. Jr., and von Destinon, M. "Budgeting and Fiscal Management." In M. J. Barr, M. K. Desler, and Associates, *The Handbook of Student Affairs Administration* (2nd ed.). San Francisco: Jossey-Bass, 2000.

Exhibit 2.1. Questions to Consider Regarding the Links Between the Institutional Budget and Your Unit.

1. Can you identify the priorities of the institution from reading the budget guidelines? What implications do those priorities have for your unit?
2. How can you maximize your budget request to link unit priorities with institutional priorities?
3. How can you determine genuine needs within your unit? Are you able to separate a need from a want as you begin to plan your budget for the coming year?
4. Do you anticipate any capital budget requests for the coming fiscal year? Has planning started within your unit for those requests?
5. What budget model is used by the institution to determine budget guidelines for the institution?
6. What expenses are anticipated for the coming fiscal year within your unit?
7. What decision-making processes are used to develop the budget for your unit? How can you respond to those processes?
8. What impact might your unit budget request have on other institutional operations?

3

The Budget Cycle(s)

BUDGET MANAGEMENT is a never-ending task for academic managers. It is not unusual for an academic manager to be supervising the current operating budget, closing the previous year's operating budget, while simultaneously making projections for the next fiscal year. If new facilities or equipment are involved that span more than one budget year, attention must also be given to capital budgets and the judicious use of reserve funds. Finally, the academic budget manager may be asked to project budgets beyond the current and next fiscal year to support the long-term financial management of the institution. Therefore, academic budget managers often feel like they are juggling several balls at the same time. This chapter will discuss the cycle of the operating budget and the budgeting processes and procedures an academic financial manager will need to understand. In addition, special attention will be given to forecasting of expenses and revenues for a unit into future fiscal years. Finally, the capital budgeting process will be discussed and special attention will be paid to auxiliary enterprise budgets.

THE FISCAL YEAR OPERATING BUDGET

Each fiscal year budget has eight distinct phases: setting institutional and unit budget guidelines, developing the unit budget request, identifying the budget implications beyond the fiscal year in question, approving the budget, monitoring budget performance, adjusting the current operating budget, closing the fiscal year, and analyzing the results. Some of the phases occur simultaneously and thus increase the sense of juggling for the budget manager.

Setting Guidelines

Budget guidelines and rules are set on the institutional level; under some circumstances, additional guidelines are also developed by departments, divisions, or programs within the institution. For example, a decision may be made to reserve some of the money allocated from the institution to a budget unit for salaries so that exceptional performers in smaller units within a school, college, or division of the university may be rewarded. By aggregating some of the personnel dollars at the school, college, or divisional level, greater flexibility is provided and small units are not adversely affected. Such an approach is permitted in most institutions for division heads, vice presidents, and deans as long as the internal rules of the unit are congruent with institutional guidelines.

Institutional Parameters

Institutional guidelines for unit or program budgets are issued early in the budgeting process. Development of institutional guidelines is not an easy process and requires financial staff to analyze past performance of the institution, the current and projected costs of utilities, and the influence of other key economic indicators (including the rate of general inflation and inflation in higher education); calculate the average return on the investment of the institution's assets; and analyze the environment around the institution, including employment and compensation patterns in the community. In large, complex, and multilayered institutions, there are many people charged with the responsibility of determining what forces outside the institution will increase or decrease revenues or influence expenses. In smaller institutions, this function is sometimes outsourced to a private consulting agency, or the expertise of one financial person is used. Although the environmental scan may be rigorous in some institutions and less so in others, each institution seeks to understand the outside forces that will inevitably impinge on the financial operation of the college or university. Those identified constraints and opportunities have a great influence on the development of institutional budget guidelines and regulations.

In addition to the external environmental scan, an analysis of past internal performance is also made. Problem units or line items, both in terms of expenses and revenues, are identified and must be accounted for in any budget rules and decisions. Large variances between the planned budget and the actual performance are studied in detail.

Finally, a strong link must be made between any planning processes in place within the institution and the budget rules. If, for example, a strategic institutional goal of reducing turnover of support staff is established, then one of the institutional budget guidelines might address compensation, benefits, or training for staff. Or if a new program initiative is to be developed as part of the institutional strategic plan, the budget guidelines must account for that resource need.

If the institution uses an incremental budgeting model, parameters are set as outside limits for spending. They are couched in "not to exceed" language. For example, "increases for travel may not exceed 2 percent." Separate decision rules usually govern personnel and other operating budget expenditures. Most institutions do not permit dollars to be transferred to and from the personnel budget within the unit. Personnel budget rules set the limit for total budget commitments in each unit for salaries and benefits for all full-time, part-time, and student employees. A separate set of guidelines focuses on general operations with some line item increases mandated, such as technology charges, while others may be lumped together for distribution within the unit. Again, limits are set regarding the amount the unit may budget as expenditures during the next fiscal year.

If the institution uses one of the other budget models, parameters will be set but only after the units are asked to project their needs for the coming year. Even under budget models that are "bottom up," institutional budget guidelines are issued and implemented prior to the final budget being approved.

It is clear that the process of developing institutional budget guidelines is based on a series of assumptions and beliefs. Budget guidelines, however they are determined, will reflect the assumptions held by planners regarding enrollment, demand for services, opportunities, and problems facing the institution. It is critical that unit budget managers understand the assumptions and beliefs that drive the budget parameters. If the unit budget manager does not understand those assumptions, clarification should be sought. Sources for clarification include the central budget office or administrative superiors. For it is only when the manager understands the rationale for guidelines that credible requests can be made for additional resources. Finally, the institutional parameters include a timetable for submission of information.

Timetables

Institutional budget instructions also include the timetable(s) for submission of all budget documents. Based on this information, each unit budget manager must establish earlier schedules for budget request submission within the unit. Institutional timetables should not be ignored, and every effort should be made to meet the institutional deadlines. If problems arise in meeting the timetable, those issues should be discussed with the appropriate budget or administrative office (dean, division, and so forth) to both inform them of the problem and determine whether there is any flexibility in deadlines. The important thing is not to ignore budget timelines for such actions can adversely affect the budget of the unit.

Developing Unit Budget Requests

There are at least ten specific steps that can assist unit budget managers in development of budget requests. Some steps can occur simultaneously and others proceed in sequential order.

Analyze Previous Unit Budget Performance

Even if you are a new budget manager it is important to carefully analyze the prior budget performance of the unit. Did the unit end the last fiscal year and prior years with a surplus or deficit? Is there a pattern of overexpenditure in some line items? If so, why? Are there some line items that consistently have a surplus at the end of the year? What is the reason for a surplus? These questions and others help the budget manager understand what occurred in the past and whether there are chronic fiscal problems or issues within the unit. Frank and open discussion should be held with members of the unit as well as the central budget office regarding the reasons behind apparent anomalies in the previous budget(s) of the unit. This analysis will also help prepare the budget manager to ask focused questions when developing the unit budget request for the next fiscal year.

Share Information

Budgeting is not a secret process, although it appears that way on some campuses. Information regarding the parameters established by the institution and the rationale for those budget rules should be shared widely within the unit. Faculty and staff need to understand why certain decisions were made. Sometimes faculty and staff will disagree with the reasons for a specific budget guideline or feel that their situation is unique and falls outside those institutional parameters. When such attitudes surface, sharing information can be a frustrating task for the budget manager. But Woodard and von Destinon (2000) indicate that information sharing stimulates all members of the organization to think creatively about solutions to ongoing fiscal issues.

Establish an Internal Process

The internal budget process within the unit should be clear to everyone involved in budget development. It is rare when one person assumes sole authority for making all budget decisions within a unit. Most often, a budget committee is formed within the unit to help inform the unit head, budget manager, or both regarding fiscal decisions. Although the ultimate responsibility for the budget remains with the unit head or budget manager, wider participation in budget issues helps inform decisions.

Once a process is established it should be followed. Nothing frustrates people more than trying to play by "the rules" and then discovering exceptions have been made for other individuals or subunits within the organization. As part of the unit budget process, additional internal guidelines may be set for all program areas. For example, if travel support is a source of frustration, then a multiyear review of travel expenditures will assist in establishing a rationale for travel support and will influence distribution to that line in the budget.

Listen

It is essential to provide an opportunity for members of the organization to be heard regarding their needs and wants both before and during the budget preparation process. Depending on the size and complexity of the unit, formal hearings or informal conversations can be held. The important task is to provide an opportunity for members of the organization to express their hopes, dreams, and aspirations for the coming year(s) and to assure them that those ideas are seriously considered by the budget manager and other decision makers within the unit. Hearings should not be pro forma but should instead provide an opportunity to explore "what if" scenarios with persons responsible for implementation. To illustrate, perhaps a program manager indicates that in order for the program to succeed a new staff person must be added. Through the process of listening, determine what will *not* occur if the new position is *not* approved and find out what other alternatives might be explored to meet the documented need, including use of graduate students, student workers, or outsourcing.

Finally, the process of having conversations and hearings regarding dreams, aspirations, wants, and needs does not have to wait until formal budget guidelines are issued by the institution. In fact, early conversations about such aspirations may make the budget development process move forward in a much more efficient and effective manner.

Establish Internal Guidelines and Timetables

As indicated earlier, the budget timetable for the unit will need to be implemented much earlier than that for the institution. The budget manager should develop an internal timeline for submission of budget materials (including new proposals) that permits review of both the short-term and long-term implications of the budget request.

Unit budget guidelines should detail the decision parameters of each line item or categories of line items in the budget. Such guidelines should easily inform those expected to develop budget proposals about the form for submission, the limits on submissions, the expectation for justification documentation, and so forth. The guidelines need not be lengthy, but they must be clear and easy to understand. As part of the unit budget guidelines, a clear invitation should be issued for those who have questions to ask them and to seek clarification of issues prior to beginning work on the budget. Such an approach saves both time and energy on the part of everyone involved in the budget process by avoiding redoing the submission materials.

Review Proposals

Requests for new funding or increased funding from programs or departments should be linked to the plan for the unit and the objectives of the institution. Each proposal should also outline the implications of the proposal beyond the fiscal year in question. What impact will the proposal have for funding in future years? The answer to that question determines the real costs to the institution.

A budget proposal should include the rationale for the request and present a clear picture of how the institution will benefit if the proposal is funded. This rationale should be stated in plain English and not be filled with jargon. Where possible, data should be provided in support of the request. It should be easy to answer questions such as, What will change as a result of the funding? What will remain the same? How many people will be served? And how will success be measured?

In addition, if anticipated savings are part of the funding proposal, examine the proposal very carefully. Are the savings real? Off-loading a program to another unit or agency might save money for the department getting rid of the program, but there is no real savings for the institution. Further, a proposal to reallocate funds to other purposes through elimination of a program should be very carefully evaluated. The question of whether the program can be eliminated must be answered, for if it is politically impossible to eliminate an old program to support a new effort, then the savings are not real. Such problems must be identified and assessed early in the budget development process.

The basic arithmetic of the proposal should also be carefully checked. Arithmetical errors happen all the time and should be identified and rectified prior to forwarding any budget proposal.

Finally, routine inflationary cost increases should not be just accepted, even if they are consistent with the general guidelines from the institution. Review of all budget increase requests should be made and the underlying assumptions for the increase should be tested. Auxiliary enterprises provide some of the best examples of the need for such testing. For example, cost increases for utilities have risen sharply in recent years. The institutional environmental scan, as well as information from the electric company, identifies the percentage of increase for the coming fiscal year. The easy way to build the budget is to apply the rate increase percentage to the current budgeted line item for electricity, but that is probably not the most accurate approach and may present a false picture. The budget analysis discussed earlier in this chapter should provide data on what the actual cost for electricity has been, and an average cost over the last three years can be calculated. The calculated figure then becomes the base for applying the anticipated increase for electricity in the new fiscal year. Other approaches could also be used, including taking the highest use year and projecting costs with an inflation factor into the current fiscal year. It may mean that these calculations will result in a savings in the line item for electricity. But it might also mean that electricity costs should be budgeted at a higher level than is approved in the institutional budget guidelines. If that is the case, then the difference can either be met through reallocation or relief can be sought from the institution.

A word of caution is in order here. Before a complete budget review in a unit occurs, a decision should be made whether the process itself will be cost effective. In other words, could the budget manager spend his or her time in more productive ways? Most budget managers review only a few key line items or object codes in a given fiscal year because of time constraints unless they are operating under a zero-based budgeting model.

Review Options

It is an axiom that there is never enough money to meet all requests at the department or unit level or for the institution. When there is a shortfall between requests and income, the easy answer is just to say no and move on. A strategic budget manager, however, should test the feasibility of other options. Those options might include developing a source of revenue to support the new program or service. Another option might be to eliminate or curtail a current program or activity in order to start a new initiative. This option must be carefully examined to assure that other units within the institution will not be adversely influenced by such a decision. Dickeson's volume *Prioritizing Academic Programs and Services* (1999) provides a well-developed discussion on how to prioritize program initiatives.

A third approach is to carefully examine whether cost savings could be captured by changing the way business is done within the unit. To illustrate, one approach might be to change the means of communicating to students in the department from traditional letters to e-mail. Another approach might be to examine whether some full-time positions could be modified to part-time or whether twelve-month positions could be converted to academic-year positions without affecting services to faculty, staff, and students. Ask the members of the department to suggest what might be done in order to garner savings to start a new program. Their creativity may be surprising and may help identify resources to start a new venture.

Provide Feedback

Improvement of the quality of requests and the accuracy of submitted budget documents will only occur if there is feedback to the individuals making the budget proposal. If the proposal review results in a decision not to forward the proposal, specific feedback about the reasons why the proposal was not forwarded should be provided to those who prepared the request. It is only through such feedback that the people involved can improve their work and future proposals. If a proposal cannot be funded at the level requested but can be supported at some lower level, then information sharing is also critical. Many new programs fail because budget managers make unilateral decisions of what can be eliminated or modified in a new program initiative. The person who made the proposal should be consulted regarding where cost savings can be made that will least influence the ultimate desired outcome of the new initiative.

If changes and adjustments are made in other line items, feedback should also be provided regarding the rationale for those changes. An informed program manager can be more effective in managing fiscal resources as well as people and programs.

Prepare Final Budget Submission(s)

After the final budget request decisions are made at the unit level (including strategies for reallocation and cost savings), it is time to prepare the final budget request documents. Properly prepared budget documents submitted to the central budget office in a timely fashion will receive the warranted attention. Submissions that are difficult to read, are sloppily done, or do not provide all the requested information probably will not be considered as carefully or positively. Follow the guidelines carefully and ask for clarification if there is uncertainty regarding the form or substance of the budget request.

Implications

One of the most common mistakes made by budget managers is to not clearly identify the implications of the budget request beyond the current fiscal year. For example, a unit submits a proposal for federal funds to support community service learning opportunities for undergraduate students. Part of the grant request might include creation of new positions as well as providing matching funds from the institution. Legitimate questions that should be asked when approval is sought for a grant proposal are: What will happen when the grant expires? How will the program be institutionalized? What are the potential costs for institutionalization of the program?

Or a request may be made for additional faculty positions. Such a proposal requires an addition to the base budget of the department, including salary and benefits. But there are also other costs associated with a new faculty position, and those must be accounted for in the budget request. Such hidden costs might include funding for space, equipment, supplies, and money for additional support staff. Requests are more likely to be considered if data clearly support the need and it is clear that the department understands and appreciates the long-term ramifications of the request beyond salary and benefits. (See Exhibit 3.1.)

Approving the Budget

The budget approval process is iterative. It is very unusual for a budget request to be submitted for approval without additional information being sought or hearings held. The budget manager might think the work is done when the budget request is submitted, but it is not. Often there will be requests from the central budget office or the review committee for clarification of certain items. In addition, it is not unusual for a proposal to be returned for modification. Everyone involved should understand that all budget requests will not and cannot be funded. Lack of funding does not necessarily mean that the program or idea has no merit. It may merely mean that other priorities were funded as opposed to the unit request.

Once the budget is created (from unit requests as modified), it is presented to the governing board for approval. This process is not automatic and may contain surprises both positive and negative. Usually a great deal of communication occurs prior to presenting the final budget documents to the governing board. The institutional parameters are discussed and agreed upon by the governing board and the institutional administration prior to campus distribution. Enrollment projections are agreed upon as well as the investment strategy, and the spending rules for the income from investment of the endowment must also have governing board approval. In addition, the board audit committee may raise questions about the performance of certain units or income or deficit projections. Final budget approval from the governing board only occurs after a long process of information sharing and decision making on the part of the board or its committees and the institutional administration.

Exhibit 3.1. Questions Regarding Development of the Unit Budget Request.

1. Have you carefully analyzed the budget performance of the unit for the last few fiscal years?
2. Do you share budget information, as appropriate, with others within the unit?
3. Have you established and discussed the process for determining the unit budget?
4. Have you listened to the wants and needs of unit members throughout the year?
5. Are internal budget guidelines and timetables developed, discussed, and distributed to members of the unit who must respond?
6. Have you carefully reviewed budget proposals from members of the unit?
7. Have you reviewed options and alternatives for each request with the person presenting the proposal?
8. Have you provided clear and direct feedback to the person who made the proposal?
9. Have you consolidated unit requests and prepared the final budget submission for the unit? Have all assumptions and computations been checked?
10. Are you able to identify the implications of the unit budget request for the unit and for other parts of the institution?

Monitoring Performance

After the budget is approved and the fiscal year begins, the budget must be monitored. Remember this must be done even when you are in the midst of preparing budget materials for the next fiscal year. In an ideal world, monitoring budget performance would be an easy task. Each month the expenses charged against the accounts in the unit would be equal to one-twelfth of the operating budget approved for the unit. If expenses proved to be more than one-twelfth of the budget, then the budget manager would immediately know whether there is a problem. Unfortunately, the world of the budget manager is far from ideal. Rarely are expenses equally divided from month to month, and errors may be made in both accounting and billing.

The diligent budget manager monitors budget performance each and every month by reviewing all the budget reports. In order to be effective at that task, the budget manager must understand both the ebb and flow of the budget and the institutional rules governing accounting and charges. What information should the budget manager review prior to raising concern about budget performance? Any number of factors could cause a problem in the budget report. For example, are salaries for faculty and staff automatically encumbered for the entire academic or fiscal year? Are those encumbrances accurate in terms of the agreed upon salary and the length of each employee's term of employment? If encumbrances are used to protect personnel dollars in the budget, then personnel expenses in the early months of the fiscal year might appear to be alarmingly high but are not really a cause for concern.

Or the budget might contain an allocation for a major piece of equipment. If that is true, then the dollars to support the purchase order for the equipment may have been encumbered in the budget although the equipment has not yet arrived.

Finally, are there known expenses that will not be charged to the budget until much later in the fiscal year? For example, does the unit sponsor a summer research program? If so, money must be reserved to support that program within the budget. Each unit will have unique expenses and unique questions that must be asked in a preliminary review of the accounting statements. The questions outlined above are merely illustrative of the type of analysis that should be used as probes by the budget manager to determine whether there is a problem that must be understood. Once the answers to these types of broad questions are clear, it is time to dig into the monthly budget report. All expense or revenue lines that are not congruent with the budget plan need to be carefully examined.

To illustrate, if the approved budget for office supplies is $10,000 for the entire fiscal year and $5,000 is charged against that office supply line in the first-month budget report, questions need to be raised. There could be any number of reasons that the charges against the office supply line are $5,000. It could be that the vendor billed the unit twice for the same order. Or it might be the case that an enterprising staff member bought supplies for an entire year because of a deep discount for bulk purchases. Or perhaps the cost of a new computer was charged against the office supply line rather than the line item supporting equipment purchases. A final reason might be that the person responsible for ordering supplies paid absolutely no attention to the budget. Each of these reasons requires a different response by the budget manager. Billing errors can be corrected, accounting entries can be reversed, initiative on the part of the enterprising staff member can be praised, and the person ignoring the limitations of the budget must be confronted. In order to stay on top of the budget, every line item should be reviewed with a high degree of specificity.

Further, if the unit relies on multiple sources of revenue to help meet the expense budget, then review of revenue performance against revenue goals should also be routine. If it appears that revenues are falling below expectations, then a number of issues should be reviewed before any action is taken. For example, is the shortfall in revenue related to an activity that will occur later in the fiscal year? Or if the revenue is from mandatory fees, is the amount in the budget congruent with enrollment figures? Only when the answers to those questions have determined that there is a genuine revenue shortfall should action be taken.

Adjusting the Current Budget

If there is a revenue shortfall, then expenses, where possible, should be adjusted downward to cover at least part of the projected deficit. For example, a freeze could be placed on ordering new equipment until the shortfall problem is resolved. Another strategy is to determine whether there are other sources of income that might be increased or identified to meet part of the budget need. In either case, a significant shortfall should not be ignored but highlighted and communicated to the administrative unit responsible for overseeing the department. Ignoring such problems will only compound the difficulty in addressing the issue.

Finally, if there are uncontrollable costs being faced by the unit, then these problems must also be identified and communicated. Examples of such unforeseen costs might be a midyear rate increase for sewer or water services or an increase in the rates for workers' compensation that was not even on the horizon when the budget was prepared and approved. These kinds of problems are issues that cannot be solved by the unit budget manager alone. They have implications for the entire institution, and decision makers and financial staff need to partner with unit budget managers in solving the problem.

When a strategy is developed to address the problem, adjustments may be made to the current fiscal year budget. One strategy might involve transferring money to the operating budget from a reserve account. Another strategy might involve transferring money from a different line item within the unit. Institutional rules and accounting practices will influence whether or not actual adjustments are made in the official institutional budget. If the printed or on-line budget is not adjusted, then the prudent manager should document any agreement with the central budget office for the record. Such documentation will serve as a reminder of the problem and the agreed upon solution at the close of the fiscal year.

Closing

To close the budget means that no more activity may be charged against or revenue added to the budget for that fiscal year. Invoices for goods and services not paid by the time of closing may be charged against the budget for the next fiscal year. If these items are substantial there could be an adverse effect on budget performance in the next fiscal year.

In order to try to minimize some of these issues many institutions have established three key dates related to the closing of the fiscal year. The first relates to the last day that new purchase orders can be processed against the current budget. Usually, that date is three to four weeks prior to the end of the fiscal year. This regulation reduces the number of outstanding purchase orders (invoices) at the close of the fiscal year. The second date relates to the beginning of the new fiscal year. It is the date when all budget expenses and revenue will be charged to the new fiscal year. This date may be prior to the actual calendar date for the fiscal year to begin. The last date is the final closing date for the budget from the previous fiscal year.

Most often the final closing date is set one month after the calendar close of the fiscal year. Known by some as the thirteenth month, this extended closing date permits larger invoices to clear and not be charged against the new fiscal year. If an institution uses the thirteenth month strategy, then there are usually limitations on the amount and type of charges and income that may be posted during the thirteenth-month period against the prior fiscal year. The thirteenth month or an extended final close of the budget year provides a much more accurate picture of the performance against both the broader institutional and unit budgets. Expenses and revenue related to a fiscal year are posted in that year. Only then can the determination be made whether the institution finished the fiscal year with a positive or negative budget balance. The effective budget manager knows and complies with these varied closing dates and understands the protocols of the institution regarding closing.

Analyzing the Results

When the budget cycle for the fiscal year is completed, the results must be analyzed. Earlier in this chapter, it was noted that the first step in the budget cycle was to analyze past performance. That is also the last step in the budget cycle and is essential for success in budget management.

Unit budget managers should take the initiative to analyze the budget performance of their unit. This will allow the budget manager to answer questions about what happened and why it happened. If the budget plan failed to meet expectations or exceeded expectations, the reason(s) for the performance must be identified. The pattern could be repeated if the causes are unknown. Questions should be asked regarding whether the performance was an anomaly or whether a trend can be identified in cost increases for certain line items that should be addressed in future budgets.

The answers to these and other questions will help the budget manager be better prepared to develop future budgets and also to answer any inquiries about past budget performance. (See Figure 3.1.)

While unit managers are analyzing results and determining causation, an analysis is also going forward at the institutional level. Depending on the size and complexity of the institution such an analysis may be quite detailed and time consuming or it may be provided at a more gross level of review. In either case, the end result of the institutional budget analysis will initially result in two types of data: a report on the results of the year and an analysis of the variance in performance from the budget plan.

Reporting results is fairly straightforward and answers the question of how the institution or the units performed during the last fiscal year. Did the institution deficit spend? Were all transfers to reserves made before the end of the fiscal year? Were all of the debt obligations met? What was the final outcome for the year, and did it result in a positive or a negative balance? Once the institution determines that the financial data are correct, then a report is prepared by the institution and reviewed by external auditors. The governing board, the administration, government agencies, and other funding sources use the final audited report of performance to understand the financial status of the institution. The purpose of the external audit is not to analyze budget performance but to assure that the fiscal data are accurate and that the institution followed proper procedures and accounting standards over the last fiscal year. The audited financial report evaluates performance data from the prior fiscal year to the fiscal year under review for purposes of comparison. But an audited financial report does not provide the critical data needed for governance and administration of the institution.

In contrast, the internal institutional budget analysis focuses on the variance between the budget plan and what actually happened over the last fiscal year. This analysis of the variance between the planned budget and actual performance helps place the budget performance for the recently ended fiscal year within the context of the performance of the prior year and the budget plan for the next fiscal year. Once variances in performance are identified, the analysis focuses on the causes of the variance. It is at this point that the individual unit analysis conducted by the unit

Figure 3.1. A Typical Budget Unit Cycle.

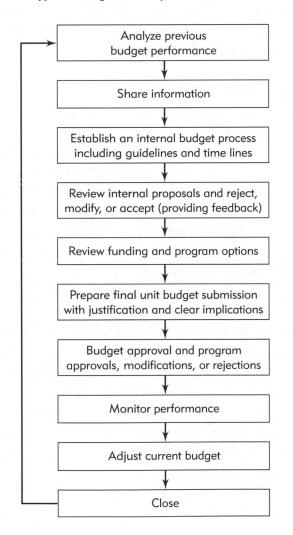

budget manager is very valuable. Usually, budget managers are the individuals in the organization who can explain why there was a difference between the planned budget and actual performance. While some variances such as an unanticipated increase can be easily explained at the institutional level, many require information from unit budget managers.

Once the institutional analysis is completed (including the explanation of variance between performance and the planned budget), a report is prepared for the governing board, key administrators, and budget managers. This report will provide guidance on monitoring the budget in the new fiscal year and may identify areas where adjustments need to be made in the current budget in order to more closely reflect the reality of revenue and expenditures faced by the institution.

Forecasting Expenses and Revenues

Often the unit budget manager will be asked to assist the institutional budget office in forecasting outcomes for the current budget year and beyond. This is a routine part of the planning process, and unit budget managers should be prepared to share their best thinking about what the current fiscal year will look like and what the future might bring. Forecasting is, at best, an inexact process, so a word of caution is in order. Revenues should be forecast as conservative figures, but expenses should not. If you forecast revenues at the highest possible level, those forecasts are often accepted and incorporated into the planning process. If the forecasted revenue goal is then not met, there may be consequences that will influence the budget future of your unit.

Forecasting for the current fiscal year is a great deal easier than projecting revenue and expenses several years into the future. The prior budget analysis conducted by the unit budget manager will provide valuable information. How has the organization done in the past? Have there been great variances between the budget plan and the final budget outcome? In addition, if the current fiscal year budget is being monitored and reviewed each month, the unit budget manager is aware of any problems that may influence the bottom line for the unit and can use that information as part of the end of the year forecast.

Forecasting beyond the current fiscal year becomes more inexact. A multiple year forecast should be based on past experience and performance of the unit. Further, the forecast should be closely linked to the planning process within the unit and the institution. For example, if a grant is a major part of the income for the unit, what will happen when the period of the grant is completed? Are there other sources of funds? Is the unit expecting the institution to pick up those costs? Will the faculty and staff supported by the grant be terminated? These are difficult questions and cannot be answered by the budget manager alone, but they must be answered if the multiple year forecast is to be accurate.

A multiple year forecast should be based on the data regarding past performance, information from an environmental scan, and the unique issues faced by the unit. To be helpful to the institution and to the unit, a forecast should be as realistic as possible and not raise either positive or negative expectations that are not likely to occur.

In addition, when developing a forecast the budget manager must clearly communicate what the assumptions are behind the forecast. For if others do not understand the assumptions, miscommunication can occur. It usually is helpful to develop a series of "what if" scenarios when making multiple year forecasts. Those alternative scenarios help clarify assumptions and highlight concerns for future budget years.

Although inexact, budget forecasting is helpful for both individual unit budget managers and the central budget office, for it highlights both potential fiscal challenges and opportunities faced by the institution and the unit. (See Exhibit 3.2.)

THE CAPITAL BUDGETING PROCESS

The capital budget focuses on items that have a useful life to the institution longer than one year. These items can include the cost of construction of new buildings, vehicles, renovation of facilities, infrastructure needs of the institution, and issues related to grounds, sidewalks, roads, and lighting. Most of these types of projects have high price tags and cannot be financed by any one unit of the institution. The source of funds for capital budgeting will vary and may come from reserve funds, a state capital project fund, a dedicated fee, or the sale of bonds. Fund sources will not be addressed in this discussion. The focus instead will be on the responsibilities of the academic unit budget manager in preparing capital budget requests and the processes of decision making regarding allocation of the capital budget.

Creating the Program Statement

Whether the proposed project is a new facility, a building renovation, an addition to or replacement of part of the infrastructure, or a large piece of equipment, a clear statement of need is essential. In addition, a description must be provided regarding the activities associated with the project and the relationship of this request to other functions within the

---

Exhibit 3.2. The Phases of Budget Development Within an Institution.

Phase One.   *Setting institutional budget guidelines:* Are they clear? Do you understand what you must do? Where are the sources of help within the institution?

Phase Two.   *Developing and submitting the unit budget:* Do you have sufficient information? And have you checked your computations?

Phase Three.   *Approval, modification, or rejection of unit budget requests:* Do you have sufficient supporting data to answer questions and "what if" scenarios?

Phase Four.   *Monitoring the performance of each unit:* Are you regularly monitoring the budget performance of your unit?

Phase Five.   *Adjusting the current fiscal year operating budget:* Have you documented any agreements regarding adjustment to the current budget?

Phase Six.   *Closing the fiscal year:* Are all known costs accounted for? Are there any problems that should be brought to the attention of the budget office?

Phase Seven.   *Analyzing the budget performance of the unit and the institution:* What are the strengths and opportunities for improvement in your unit?

Phase Eight.   *Forecasting future expenses and revenues:* Are you clear about the assumptions in your forecasts?

institution. A good program statement allows a person unfamiliar with the project to easily understand why it is important. What will occur as a result of the project, and what needs will be met if the project is approved?

Some program statements may be very brief. For example, the program statement for a replacement of the storm sewer system in a section of the campus that frequently experiences flooding might contain information regarding current problems and losses experienced, a description of the type of system to be installed, an initial cost estimate, a description of the possible disruptions as a result of the project, a site map showing where the storm sewer will be located, and assurances that this solution will prevent flooding from occurring in the future in this part of campus.

Program statements for facility construction or renovation must be more comprehensive. In addition to identifying the need for the new building or building renovation, a detailed description of the types of activities that will take place in the facility must be provided. This description should include information on how many people will be served, what specialized facilities are needed, and any regulatory requirements that must be accommodated in the construction of the building. Information must be provided on the impact the renovation or new construction will have on the rest of the campus. Estimates of needed square footage should be provided, as well as any special requirements for finishes, heating and cooling, parking, supply delivery, and security. The program statement must provide sufficient information for decision makers to be able to understand what difference this investment will make in the life of the campus.

Finally, the program statement should outline the proposed timeline for the project. The timeline will have great implications for the development of the project financial plan.

Developing the Financial Plan

Usually the unit budget manager will need assistance in developing the financial plan for the proposed capital project. A rough construction cost estimate can be obtained by use of a consultant or by receiving help from the facility planners at the institution. Rough cost estimates are based on industry or institutional standards for the cost of constructing certain types of facilities such as offices or laboratories. Rough estimates also provide information about what factors should be included in the cost estimate for items such as site preparation, building circulation (stairwells, corridors, and emergency exits), specialized equipment, technology needs, and furnishings. These preliminary cost estimates should be calculated along with a budget contingency of approximately 10 to 15 percent of the estimated project cost. These figures, together, will provide a preliminary estimate of the cost of the project. The estimated cost is then used as the basis for a preliminary financial plan. In addition to estimated construction costs, the preliminary financial plan must also estimate the amount of money needed in outgoing fiscal years to support the project, including ongoing costs of facility operation, maintenance, and repair. Usually a unit budget manager will need assistance in developing the financial plan and must understand that this is just a preliminary estimate used to make initial decisions about the feasibility of the project.

Performing the Preliminary Review

Institutional decision makers will use the preliminary financial plan to make a preliminary decision about the feasibility of the capital project. Some institutions have a special capital planning group with representatives from the finance, budget, facilities, academic, and student services offices. On other campuses, preliminary project reviews are made by the chief financial officer, the executive officers of the institution, or the facilities department. Finally, if new construction or major renovations are involved, the appropriate governing board committee must also agree that the preliminary plans are reasonable and are congruent with the overall facility plans for the institution. However the preliminary review process is conducted, only four outcomes are possible: rejection of the proposal, a request for modification of the proposal, an appropriation for a detailed cost estimate and plan prior to approval, or outright approval of the project.

Making a Detailed Cost Estimate

A detailed and fairly accurate cost estimate for a project cannot be made without investment of time and money in the planning process. An architect or engineer must develop detailed designs and cost estimates for the proposed facility. At this critical design development stage, careful attention is paid to the site preparation needs, the quality and capacity of the institutional infrastructure supporting the project (plumbing, steam and chilled water lines, electric, gas and water, and so forth), and compliance with all applicable city and state codes including life safety needs. Furnishings and finishes are also described in detail and the actual square foot requirements for all parts of the structure are determined. Most important, the design development stage helps planners see how the elements of the project will work together to make a coherent whole. The final project cost estimate at the end of the design development stage will reflect all anticipated costs associated with the project, including but not limited to architectural and engineering fees, permits, construction costs, site preparation, equipment, furnishings, and a contingency for unexpected issues. Once that figure is determined, a decision can be made whether to move forward with the project.

Approving the Final Project

Smaller projects may not require a design development stage and are approved or rejected at initial submission of the idea. Whether or not design development is required, final project approval must be congruent with institutional goals and priorities. The capital budgeting process does not differ from the operating budget in that there is never enough money to fund all requests. Therefore, the capital plan supports established priorities for both the immediate and long-term capital funding by the institution.

Top priority in capital budgeting must be given for projects that address documented health (asbestos removal) and safety (fire alarm, sprinkler systems) needs. Changes required by law or government regulations (which have the force of law) must also be funded. Examples of legal requirements that have capital budget implications include but are not limited to: research animal safety regulations, facility and parking access for the mobility impaired, and handling of hazardous waste. Each of these issues can have a large price tag that must be accounted for in the capital budgeting process.

As a second priority, capital projects are approved that support and enhance current program activities within the institution. Space to accommodate teaching, research, office, and laboratory programs, as well as space to support current student programs and activities, fall into this priority for funding. Examples might include a new faculty office building that brings faculty together from related departments or a new residence hall for undergraduate students.

The third priority for capital funding is initiatives that are new. These are the types of projects that aid in advancing the institution to the next higher level. Examples might include a building to house a new academic center for the social sciences or the addition of a 1,500-seat performance hall or the redevelopment of outdoor space to make it more attractive for recreation and leisure. These are exciting projects and usually must be closely related to fund-raising activities for the capital outlay is enormous. But when they are developed and implemented, such capital projects can bring a whole new level of excitement to the institution.

Whatever the priority of the project, if approved, it must be linked to a comprehensive financial plan. Even if a gift supports a major portion of the cost of the facility or renovation, new facilities are a major ongoing commitment on the part of the institution. Operating and maintaining the facility will have budget implications over the life of the building, as will repairs and eventual renovation. All of these factors must be considered as part of the financial plan for any capital project. (See Exhibit 3.3.)

THE SPECIAL CASE OF AUXILIARIES

Auxiliary enterprises, as noted earlier in this volume, are self-sustaining components of the institution that "stand on their own bottom." The auxiliary is responsible for generating the income needed to provide for all the expenses associated with running the auxiliary operation. These expenses include all costs of operation (including salaries and benefits), all debt service, and indirect costs paid to the institution. Most important, auxiliary enterprises are expected to develop sufficient reserve funds to cover the cost of repair and renovation of facilities. Usually a new building is expected to be financed from revenue, gifts, and money borrowed either from the institution or through issuing bonds.

Most often auxiliary enterprises are located in intercollegiate athletic units or in the division of student affairs and include items such as residence halls, residential colleges, recreation buildings, arenas, stadiums, outdoor recreation space, and student centers. Even though an auxiliary enterprise is self-supporting, budget managers must comply with the capital planning and approval processes on the campus.

Reserve Funds

Each auxiliary enterprise must develop reserve funds to cover the cost of repair, replacement, renovation, new construction, or revenue shortfalls. Some institutions require several reserve funds dedicated to items such as painting or construction. Others have one reserve fund for the entire auxiliary unit. In order to develop reserve funds, money must be transferred to reserve funds from the operating budget each year. Although such transfers are not usually mandatory, the wise budget manager should consider reserve transfers as a cost of doing business. Failure to transfer to reserves will result in a dearth of money to handle much needed facility upgrades

---

Exhibit 3.3. Questions Regarding the Unique Case of Capital Budgeting.

1. Does the program statement developed by your unit provide a clear statement of need within the context of the institution? Does the program statement clearly outline the activities that will take place or be enhanced by new facilities or equipment?
2. Have you obtained a preliminary cost estimate, including estimates for construction, furnishings, equipment, and technology support?
3. Have you factored in debt service as part of your financial plan if that is necessary?
4. Has the project received preliminary approval by appropriate decision makers or is more work needed?
5. Have you received funding for preparation of detailed cost estimates, program description, and actual plans?
6. Has the time line for the project been developed and the budget implications of that time line explained?
7. Does the financial plan account for both annual repair and maintenance and long-term repair, renovation, or replacement?

and emergencies. The financial staff at the institution can help determine a reasonable percentage of the operating budget that should be transferred to reserves each year.

Excess income over expenses at the close of the fiscal year in auxiliary enterprises should also be transferred to reserves. It should be noted, however, that some institutions require that some of the excess income over expenses be transferred to the central institutional budget. The wise auxiliary budget manager should have a plan in hand for repairs and renovations that makes the case for the entire amount to be left in the auxiliary enterprise reserve account.

New Construction

To illustrate, as part of the strategic plan of the institution the need for additional undergraduate housing has been identified. A program statement is developed outlining the size of the facility, the kinds of space that will be part of the structure, the mix of single and double rooms, kitchen facilities, and other common spaces. Approval is given to seek outside funding in partial support of the new construction. With the initial program statement in hand, the development office solicits a naming gift of $4 million for the new residential unit. Simultaneously, the design development phase of the project is moving forward and a more accurate cost estimate is developed.

The new cost estimate is used to develop a financial plan for construction of the residence hall with the following assumptions. The $4 million gift will be paid in four equal installments of $1 million beginning in the current fiscal year and for three years thereafter. The room rental rates for the building will be adjusted annually at a rate of 4.0 percent. The occupancy rate for the building, when it is completed, will be 92 percent during the regular academic year and 50 percent during the months of June, July, and August. Operating costs for the building (including utilities) are estimated to increase on an average of 3.5 percent per year. The building budget must contribute to the reserve fund for ongoing repair and maintenance of all residence halls after year five of operation. When all of these assumptions are modeled, the detailed financial plan can indicate when the building will become completely self-supporting, how long other residential units must subsidize the cost of initial construction, or even if the size of the building will permit reduction of the construction debt in a timely manner.

Each assumption, building size, and building amenity can be added or subtracted from the financial plan or adjusted in some way. Many iterations of the financial plan will be developed until all decision makers are satisfied that the building as planned is financially feasible. Only then may the project go forward.

Repair and Renovation

Each auxiliary enterprise must also develop a long-term repair and renovation plan for the facilities in its area. The plan is usually two-fold. First is the identification of cyclical expenses such as painting, routine equipment and furniture replacement, and carpeting. Such cyclical expenses should be identified and a replacement schedule identified for each type of expense. These routine expenses can either be funded as part of the operating budget or become a special funding category from reserve accounts of the auxiliary.

Second is the major repair and renovation schedule, including items such as roof replacement, tuck-pointing, HVAC systems, major facility renovation, upgrades of electrical, plumbing, and air handling systems, and so forth. These items require a multiyear plan and schedule that serves as a capital facilities plan for the auxiliary unit. If the auxiliary has responsibility for oversight of many facilities, such plans can be quite elaborate and very expensive. Development of the plan is a time consuming process and should involve representatives of the facilities office, the auxiliary unit, and the budget office. Sometimes an outside consultant is hired to assess the state of the facilities and recommend priorities for major repairs and renovation. Whether or not an outside consultant is used, projects should be prioritized within the auxiliary unit. The same protocols that apply for the institutional capital budget are also used here; issues of legal compliance and health and safety receive the top priority for funding. Such multiyear repair and renovation plans must also be approved by the appropriate decision-making body at the institution.

The differences between auxiliary units and other parts of the institution are in the source of the funds and the lack of support from the capital budget for major repairs and renovations. The same rigor and planning is required in auxiliaries as in other parts of the institution.

SUMMARY

Several budget cycles influence the work of the unit budget manager. Operating budgets, capital budgets, and auxiliary enterprises all have regulations governing processes and procedures. Understanding the ebb and flow of the budget process within the institution can help make the work of the manager easier. Finally, budget managers should ask for assistance from the financial staff if they have questions or if a project is complex and difficult.

REFERENCES

Dickeson, R. C. *Prioritizing Academic Programs and Services: Reallocating Resources to Achieve Strategic Balance.* San Francisco: Jossey-Bass, 1999.

Woodard, D. B. Jr., and von Destinon, M. "Budgeting and Fiscal Management." In M. J. Barr, M. K. Desler, and Associates, *The Handbook of Student Affairs Administration* (2nd ed.). San Francisco: Jossey-Bass, 2000.

Problems and Pitfalls in Fiscal Management

BECAUSE BUDGETING and fiscal management are inexact processes at best, problems and unanticipated issues do occur. If, however, the academic budget manager is able to anticipate most problems and develop solutions, then the unusual or the unexpected will be much easier to handle. This chapter is designed to help budget managers avoid common problems and pitfalls that face individuals with fiscal management responsibility.

What are the most important issues that a new budget manager must face? What are the common problems in budgeting and financial management? How can problems be avoided or minimized? What advice might be helpful to new budget managers? The advice in this chapter is drawn from the combined wisdom of a number of colleagues serving as line managers, fiscal managers, fiscal staff, and executive staff members at several institutions. It is hoped that their collective wisdom will aid unit budget managers in becoming more effective in their role. Finally, the chapter closes with a discussion of attitudinal issues that may get in the way of effectiveness in fiscal management.

COMMON ISSUES

There are a number of common issues facing new budget managers in any institution of higher education. Among them are understanding the organization, understanding your "inheritance," assessing capabilities, identifying problems and developing solutions, and managing change.

Understanding the Organization

In order to function effectively, a new budget manager needs to understand both the unit and the larger institution. Such understanding does not come easily and involves both initiative and time. Most managers understand that learning about their unit is extremely important. Understanding internal procedures, decision-making structures, and the way business is currently done in the unit is a first step toward success. But paying attention only to the unit can be a trap. Often new budget managers get so caught up in learning the day-to-day operations within their unit that important connections are not made to the larger institution.

It is important to get out of the office and meet people across the institution who are essential to the success of your unit. Each unit is different, but key contacts to make include individuals in accounting, budgeting, purchasing, technical support, and physical plant. Becoming more than a voice on the phone is invaluable if there are problems to be solved or information is needed.

In addition to getting answers to specific questions, these contacts provide valuable "soft data" that can assist you in budget management. Ask questions about past practices of your unit: What worked well? What frustrated others both within and without the unit?

Finally, a network of colleagues across the institution helps new budget managers set reasonable expectations for others within their own unit and in the institution. For example, how long does it really take to get a purchase order processed or a budget transfer made? Who should you really call if you find an accounting mistake? Answers to such questions will help a budget manager approach tasks in a much more efficient and effective manner.

Understanding Your "Inheritance"

Each budget manager approaches the task in a unique way and develops internal processes and structures that fit with his or her management style and approach to problem solving. For success, it is essential that new budget managers understand what mores regarding the budget and financial management were formerly part of the organization. Such information helps new budget managers avoid making assumptions about policies, procedures, and people. Some units have a history of tight central control with all expenditures approved by the unit budget manager. Others have a system where expenditures can be made up to a certain dollar amount without the approval of the budget manager. Such practices have become ingrained in the organizational culture and if budget managers do not understand what was in place prior to their arrival, there is great potential for miscommunication and confusion. To illustrate, a new budget manager received central budget materials and developed additional budget guidelines for the program directors within her department. At a meeting of all the program directors, the budget guidelines and back-up information were distributed. The new budget manager looked around the table and saw consternation on the faces of the program directors. As the budget manager questioned the reaction, she discovered that the department heads had never before been asked to participate in building the budget. A great deal of additional assistance was needed to help department heads prepare budget materials during that initial year. If the new budget manager had understood the history of the division, preparation could have occurred earlier in the year and training implemented to help department heads deal with this new expectation.

Your "inheritance" as a budget manager also means gaining a full understanding of all accounts and revenue sources that are part of the financial plan for the unit. Again, assumptions should not be made about the validity of the current budget or the uses made for reserve funds. Examine the financial records and ask questions so that you can pinpoint problems and issues prior to the time they become major concerns. For example, perhaps your examination reveals that there is always a substantial variance between the budgeted line item for computer supplies and the actual expenditures in that line. That should be a flag to alert you to discover the reason for the variance. If you get a response that "we have always done it that way—just transfer funds from another line to cover it" then you know that you have a budget problem that must be solved.

Understanding your "inheritance" also means that you will be able to create a list of issues that must be addressed and problems that must be solved. Priorities for addressing the issues involved can then be established. All issues cannot be addressed in one fiscal year, but progress can be made. In addition, processes and procedures that work can be identified and continued. Spending time understanding what you inherited prepares you to become a much better budget manager.

Assessing Capabilities

As a budget manager, you must be able to effectively assess the capabilities of your colleagues in the area of finance. For some units, the budget is straightforward and easy to manage, and support needs for the budget manager are minimal. In other units, managing the budget involves multiple accounts and sources of revenue as well as reserve funds and capital projects. As unit budget manager you will need to assess the capabilities of your colleagues in handling financial matters. Are there individuals in the unit who handle purchasing and other routine financial matters very well? Are there individuals who cannot seem to focus on matters financial? Each of your colleagues will have strengths and weaknesses, and a judgment of skills and capability must be made prior to granting anyone financial authority. Who among your colleagues expresses interest in finance and budgeting? Who among your colleagues is open to new ideas and change? If there is interest and openness, a bright and competent person can be trained in fiscal matters and become an asset to the entire organization.

In addition, you must assess your own capabilities and identify your strengths and opportunities for improving your performance. Even if there are not formal staff development programs on matters of budget and finance, wise managers identify what they need to know and seek help from others within the institution to acquire the needed skill, information, or competency.

Identifying Problems and Developing Solutions

As discussed earlier in this volume, perhaps the greatest skill that a financial manager can have is the ability to anticipate real problems before they become crisis situations. Regular and routine budget reviews are invaluable in the process of problem identification. In addition, a retrospective view of past budgets and performance helps pinpoint chronic issues that must be addressed in the unit. It is important to differentiate between chronic budget problems (which require long-term solutions) and minor issues that can be addressed through immediate changes in policies and procedures.

Chronic budget and financial problems will not be easily solved. For example, one program within a department goes consistently into debt because the budget to support the program is unrealistic. Other programs and general line items within the department have been used to cover the program deficit, but as general costs rise and resources shrink this strategy is less and less viable. Further, the chronic deficit has reduced the amount of money available to be transferred to equipment reserves for use by the entire department. This state of affairs represents a chronic problem. Because the pattern has been firmly established that the program in question can overspend their budget allocation, there are both negative attitudes and fiscal realities to confront. In this case, the unit budget manager must develop both a short-term and a long-term approach to solving the problem. The short-term solution might be to discuss the overspending issue with the program director and jointly establish a target-spending figure that will reduce overspending in the program. The long-term solution might be to submit a special budget request for additional support presenting evaluation data of unit effectiveness. Another solution might be to assess all program offerings of the department to determine whether any can be dropped, modified, or consolidated. A third solution might be to ask the program staff to generate ideas to assure that budget performance within the program improves. A fourth solution might involve developing a new revenue source for the unit. Each of these strategies needs to be tested within the unit and cannot be adopted unilaterally. Consultation must be held with appropriate colleagues in the institution regarding both the intended and unintended consequences of the strategy.

If the problem is a chronic one, then the unit budget manager will also need to seek assistance from the staff in central budget office. Lay out the problem and alternate solutions and ask them for their input and advice on the best solution for the particular issue. Their broad-based expertise will be enormously helpful in solving the issues you face. The best approach is to be forthright about the problem and not to ignore it. If you are clear and direct, you will establish important credibility with the central budget office that will be useful for years to come.

When problems occur, the relationships the wise budget manager has developed provide great resources. Others who have faced similar issues can share their wisdom and expertise with you. You, in turn, can eventually help others develop plans to address issues that they face. One of the key requisites for management success is to discover what other people did under similar circumstances and what the pattern of response was to those decisions.

Managing Change

One of the most difficult issues that a manager faces is the management of change. Whether the proposed change is large or small, it is guaranteed to create resistance and concern within the budget unit. Barr and Golseth (1990) developed three guiding principles for managing change that are particularly useful for the financial manager: determining issues of agreement and commonality, demonstrating integrity, and demonstrating utility (pp. 209–210).

The principle of establishing commonality is particularly important in managing fiscal change. What are the issues that frustrate people within the organization? What is working well? What needs to be modified? Broad and open discussions within the budget unit will reveal common questions of concern and also identify those processes and procedures that do not need to be fixed. Such dialogue should be continuous within the budget unit, for consistent problem solving will stop small problems from becoming a crisis. Finally, if people become invested in the process of developing solutions and their input is valued, they are much more likely to support change.

Integrity is essential to a positive change strategy within a budget unit. Demonstrating integrity is a simple but powerful practice that guides the ethical dimension of budget management. "Integrity involves principles that are assumed rather than affirmed. Integrity means demonstrating consistency between beliefs and actions" (Barr and Golseth, 1990, p. 210). For the budget manager, integrity in managing change is essential. Complete agreement on the changes needed is not always necessary, but everyone involved in the process of change must be treated with respect and honesty. The principle of integrity means that the budget manager must demonstrate consistency and fairness in all matters related to fiscal management.

The last principle in managing change is that of utility. Is the change worth doing? What is gained if the change is made? What is lost? Who benefits? Is it worth time and energy to address or is it making a "mountain out of a molehill"? Utility is an important principle in managing fiscal change, for often elaborate solutions to a problem are developed when it is only an anomaly and will never be repeated. Or money-saving ideas are introduced that actually cost money because of the need for record keeping. When managing change one of the first questions to ask is whether the change is really needed and whether it is worth the time and energy involved in the process. A good rule of thumb is to remember that everything works better when it is simple and easy to understand. As one financial manager indicates, the wise budget manager "works with the hand that is dealt to them and phases in change" (E. Wachtel, personal communication, July, 2001).

COMMON PITFALLS

There are a number of pitfalls that can be avoided if the budget manager is aware of them and analyzes what is going on with these concerns in mind.

Overestimating Revenue

The most common mistake of new budget managers is to overestimate revenue for the unit. Revenue estimates should always be conservative and backed up by details that clarify the assumptions for the stated revenue goal. Sometimes revenue is overestimated because the budget manager and the program staff are enthusiastic and optimistic about participation and response to a new program idea. That enthusiasm clouds the hard fiscal judgments that must be made. Sometimes one-time revenue from a seminar or conference is projected, by mistake, into the future as an ongoing revenue stream. Finally, revenue calculations can be inflated because of simple arithmetic errors or faulty assumptions about the future of the program or the amount of support that will be forthcoming from the institution. Whatever the reason, failure to accurately estimate revenue will cause problems down the road. Remember that conservative revenue estimates are the foundation of sound budgeting.

Postponing a Problem

Sometimes when taking on new budget management responsibilities, the easiest course of action seems to be to do nothing. At times that is a reasonable strategy, but often avoidance only causes the problems to grow. If there is great variance between expected budget performance for the unit and what is actually happening, then there is a problem that must be addressed. Deficits do not vanish and overexpenditures do not melt away. The astute budget manager identifies the problems and systematically tries to deal with them. Sometimes the solution can be found within the unit. Sometimes help is needed from elsewhere in the institution. Whatever is needed, the financial manager must find a solution.

Failing to Ask for Help

Fear of looking foolish is no excuse for not asking for help when it is needed. The greatest skill that a budget manager can have is recognizing an issue before it becomes a larger problem. The second greatest skill is asking for help to solve the problem. Help is available from all sorts of sources within the institution, including fellow budget managers and members of the central financial staff. Wasting time and energy on trying to solve a problem alone is not a good use of your time, and the solution you develop may not be optimal. Asking for help is simply a sound management strategy.

Failing to Identify Hidden Costs

All programs have hidden as well as visible costs. Hidden costs usually involve space and other overhead issues; when budget proposals to support new programs are presented, those hidden costs must be identified. It is only when all such costs are known that a rational decision can be made about the investment in the new project or facility. Capital budgeting requires that operational costs for new facilities be identified and accounted for in the financial plan. But it is not just new buildings or renovated facilities that have hidden costs. For example, if a new position is added to an office, more is involved than the salary and benefits for the individual involved. Questions must be asked such as the following: Is there available office space? Is new equipment needed? Is there appropriate support staff? Is reconfiguration of space necessary? The answers to these questions will determine the hidden costs of the new venture and must be considered in making a budget decision.

Failing to Plan for the End

Budget managers dealing with grant funds often encounter this pitfall. What will happen when the grant runs out? Will personnel associated with the grant be terminated? Will they be reassigned? What happens to the equipment? What are the expectations of the people involved with the grant?

When the grant is awarded, euphoria is high and it is difficult to get persons involved with the grant to engage in developing alternate scenarios for the end of the funding period. Wishful thinking that the grant will be renewed may be misplaced and a sensible plan to deal with the closing of a grant needs to be developed at the beginning of the grant period. To do otherwise means expectations for continued employment and service would rise. Planning for the end should begin at the start.

Failing to Identify Multiyear Consequences

Both people and programs change, and the wise budget manager views those changes through the lens of multiple year fiscal consequences. The question to ask is, What is likely to happen, and what will the fiscal consequences be if that scenario plays out? In fact, alternative scenarios that provide sufficient information should be developed for any new program initiative so that decision makers can make an informed decision of whether the gamble of approving the allocation is worth it. The term *gamble* is used deliberately because every new program, new hire, and new piece of equipment is a gamble for the institution. Will the new faculty member develop sufficient research grants and a national reputation in order to justify the investment in the research laboratory and graduate assistants? Will the new piece of equipment really save staff time and reduce the number of support staff needed in a unit? Providing as much information as possible to decision makers helps them make the best decisions that can be made. Part of the information that they need includes the implications beyond the current budget year.

Failing to Understand Implications for Others

There are both intended and unintended consequences for any decision. Part of the task of a unit budget manager is to minimize the unintended consequences of a decision for the entire institution. To illustrate, just because a unit has sufficient funds in the budget does not mean that those funds can be spent without regard to institutional rules, regulations, and salary guidelines. Offering a position to a staff member at a compensation level that falls outside the institutional guidelines can cause problems for other managers dealing with persons in similar positions. Using funds to purchase equipment such as espresso machines or laptop computers for everyone in the unit creates tension with other parts of the institution. Providing greater travel support than others can access causes ill will. Even if funds are available, expenditures should be in line with institutional guidelines and practices; if exceptions are made, the rationale should be clearly explained. The credibility of the unit and perhaps increased future funding is at stake.

Assuming the Good Times Will Continue

In the 1980s and 1990s, many institutional and unit budget managers were caught off guard when the traditional sources of funding for higher education began to erode. Making the assumption that budgets will constantly increase and that inflationary allocations will also be provided is a major error in budgeting. The astute budget manager should develop plans to include a downturn in the funding picture for the unit. One of the ways to plan for harder times is to build flexibility into the current operating budget of the unit. For example, building an equipment replacement line into the annual operating budget allows the budget manager to replace equipment when needed. In addition, it provides a cushion for reallocation in budget years when allocations are not as robust and redistribution of line items is needed. Building such flexibility into the budget is not an easy task, for funding for such line items must be carved out of other important line items in the budget. It will, however, permit the unit to weather reduced circumstances without major disruptions.

Becoming aware of common pitfalls permits a budget manager to test whether those mistakes have been made in the past and in current circumstances. Being forewarned permits the budget manager to be forearmed (Exhibit 4.1).

ADVICE TO NEW BUDGET MANAGERS

What insights and advice might be most helpful to new or less experienced budget managers? The following suggestions for *success* in budget and fiscal management are compiled from colleagues across the country.

Exhibit 4.1. Have You Avoided These Pitfalls in Budget Management?

1. Do you fall into the trap of overestimating revenue? What assumptions underlie your revenue figures? Can you explain them to decision makers?
2. Does your budget address long-term and chronic issues facing the unit, or are you still trying to ignore them?
3. Is there someone or some office in the institution that can assist you in addressing a long-term or chronic problem?
4. What are the hidden costs associated with each project or program within your unit? Can you identify those costs, and are they accounted for in the budget plan?
5. If you are administering a time-limited grant or contract, what plans are in place for the end of the grant?
6. What are the multiyear consequences of the budget decisions made within your unit? Are those consequences defensible?
7. What are the implications of your budget decisions beyond your specific unit?
8. Have you made the fatal error of assuming the good times will continue unabated? Have you established reserve funds for equipment, repair and renovation, or contingencies?

Ask Questions

If you are uncertain about something, ask questions. You can save a great deal of time and energy if you seek clarification early in the process rather than later. Do not let your ego get in the way of getting clarification on issues and problems. Bluffing does not work in fiscal management, and be careful not to be bluffed by others.

Be Prepared

Being prepared means doing your homework. You should have sufficient data and backup material at hand so that you can answer inquiries about expenditures and revenue. You may never be asked for such material, but you will feel more confident if you have it and can refer to data when answering questions.

Learn to Say "I Don't Know"

If you don't know the answer to a question, do not be afraid to say so but promise that you will get the answer and set a date to do so. It is refreshing for decision makers to work with people who admit when they do not have an answer to a question, and such admissions increase your credibility with others. To be effective as a fiscal manager you need to leave your ego at home.

Identify Both the Stakeholders and the Decision Makers

The stakeholders of a unit may be people very different from the decision makers regarding budget matters. Understand which people are part of each group and what influence they may have on your organization and your budget. What information can and should you share with each of these groups of important people?

Discover What Decision Makers Need

What do the individuals who make budget decisions need to know? What do they care about? What information will have the most meaning for each of the decision makers? Some people want to know comparative data from other, similar institutions. Others are interested in how the unit can contribute to the cost of the request from existing resources. (Note: this is an example of the old adage, "put your money where your mouth is!")

Still others will want to know how many people will be served. Some decision makers want to know evaluative data about unit performance. Other individuals will want to have data supporting the need for the proposal. Each person involved in the fiscal decision-making process will have different priorities. The key to becoming a successful budget and fiscal manager is to identify what information decision makers need to make informed choices about the allocation of resources and give it to them. This is not a case where one size fits all.

Don't Play Games

This advice is both for decision makers in budgeting and those making proposals. Nothing is more frustrating than having someone play games in the budget process. It expends time and energy and, when recognized, creates huge credibility problems. One of the most common games is to inflate the budget request, knowing full well that it is unrealistic but hoping that the actual amount of money needed will be allocated to the unit. The second most common game is to withhold information about pending revenue or costs associated with the program. This approach is foolish at best because the truth will eventually arise through the simple process of doing business. A third game is to only present the worst possible case scenario when requesting budget support. The reality is that the worst possible case will probably not materialize and a budget manager who employs this strategy will soon be seen as a harbinger of gloom and doom rather than a credible manager. A fourth game is to try to "hide" money. Sometimes budget managers try to "hide" money in other inflated line items or in reserve accounts. Such approaches are usually quickly uncovered and raise significant issues of honesty for the budget unit and the integrity of the budget manager. A fifth game is to attempt to politicize the budget process through involvement of one or more constituency groups. Students are often used in this process when budget managers and administrators tell them they simply do not have enough money to accommodate their request and the only way to get money is to "lobby" the administration. Rarely are good budget decisions made when they are subject to the whims of the student newspaper editorial page. The games just outlined are merely illustrative of inappropriate strategies that budget managers employ when trying to get budgetary support.

The central administration and the central budget office can also make the mistake of playing games in the development of budget guidelines and providing information to unit budget managers. Withholding information and painting a more negative budget picture than really exists are among the games sometimes played by central administration. A second game is to make the process of asking for budget support so cumbersome with many forms and required submissions that unless a unit budget manager is tenacious, discouragement will set in. A final strategy of decision makers is to delay responses to requests so that responses are not timely and funds simply cannot be spent as proposed in the current fiscal year. An example of this is withholding permission to fund a new position (and thus recruit for it) until a month prior to the academic year. It may be several months before the position is filled and, although the budget request is approved, substantial savings are accrued to the institution. Finally, the central budget office might set unrealistic deadlines for the submission of materials in support of expanded budget requests. (See Exhibit 4.2.)

Playing games is a waste of time, energy, and creativity and should be avoided by both unit budget managers and decision makers throughout the institution. Gamesmanship invites feelings of distrust and lack of confidence in the fiscal management process.

Seek Legal Advice When Needed

Contracts for goods and services and personnel issues can consume a great deal of time and energy of a unit budget manager. Consultation should be held with the legal counsel prior to signing any contract for goods and services that obligates the institution. If in-house counsel is available, contract review is relatively routine. If outside counsel is used, contract review by lawyers can become expensive. One strategy is to organize an institutionwide seminar on contracts that provides all budget managers with general information. In addition, institutional policies should limit the amount of a contract that can be signed only by a unit budget manager.

Personnel issues are extraordinarily complex and may be complicated by statutory requirements, current case law, or other regulations. If you are dealing with a problem employee, seek assistance from the human resources office or legal counsel prior to taking any action.

Be Honest

This is a corollary of the piece of advice given above but is much more powerful. It involves your personal credibility as a unit budget manager. You must be honest in your dealing with others throughout the organization. If a mistake has been made do not try to cover it up but seek good advice on how to deal with the problem and how to avoid such errors in the future. Being honest also means that you must provide straightforward feedback to unrealistic requests and proposals. Stringing people along does not make sense either in terms of their level of frustration or your credibility. Just because money is involved does not mean that ethical behavior should not prevail.

Pay Attention to Details

Sound fiscal management requires that the unit budget manager pay attention to details. Postings in accounts should be checked for accuracy. Computations should be cross-checked for arithmetical errors. An effective

---

Exhibit 4.2. Unproductive Budget Games.

Academic Budget Managers

1. Inflating the budget request beyond need.
2. Withholding information from decision makers.
3. Sharing only the worst possible scenario with decision makers.
4. Attempting to "hide" money.
5. Politicizing the budget process by getting advocates involved who are not part of the decision-making structure.

Central Budget Officers

1. Withholding important information from academic budget managers.
2. Presenting a more negative budget picture than actually exists.
3. Requiring unnecessary paperwork and complexity within the budget process.
4. Delaying responses on routine matter.
5. Setting unrealistic deadlines for budget submissions.

budget manager cannot just rely on others to provide details; periodically the unit budget manager must personally review accounts, question expenditures, and focus on long-range projections in the minute sense as well as dealing with the "big picture." Verifying details makes a difference both in credibility and effectiveness.

Make Few Initial Assumptions

Take the time to test all assumptions in proposals and in the current budget. Sometimes the historical budget of a unit is accepted as a "given" by a budget manager, and that may not be the case. The assumptions built into the base budget should be tested for accuracy on a periodic basis for both costs and needs that have changed over time. Testing those assumptions provides opportunities for reallocation of resources within the unit. Careful analysis of budget performance of the unit can help determine whether the underlying assumptions of the budget are accurate and reflect the current needs of the unit.

Also, any assumptions made in budget proposals should be clearly and explicitly stated as part of the proposal. If the proposal is based on a certain participation rate, the rate must be stated. If the proposal is time limited, that assumption should also be made very clear. Remember, however, if you are asked the question of whether additional resources will be needed in the future, do not promise more than you can deliver and learn to never say "never," because circumstances and needs change.

Effectiveness as a budget manager is as much related to how you approach your work as how you do it. This next section will highlight attitudinal issues that can get in the way of effective performance as a budget manager.

THE ATTITUDE FACTOR

A unit budget manager must be prepared to answer questions and provide data to decision makers. Immediately approaching that process as a confrontational activity is, however, a mistake. When questioned about the reasons for a request or why a certain budgetary action happened, defenses sometimes go up and the budget manager gets ready to do battle.

Questions by the budget office do not necessarily mean that your judgment is challenged but may mean that the budget office is seeking information and clarification. Assuming that you are under attack immediately places you in a defensive position in any subsequent negotiation and creates unnecessary problems for your unit.

Active involvement in the budget process is essential for an academic budget manager. Although other persons in the unit can handle the routine transactions needed to keep the operation functioning, the budget manager must truly understand what is going on. Fiscal management is an important task for an administrator. Taking the position that it is merely detail and that as an administrator you have more important things to do is an invitation to trouble. The detail is as important as the overall strategy. Disdain for involvement is not an option for the effective budget manager. One of the biggest errors that can be made by budget managers is to feel that they are too important to be involved in the detail. Taking the time to increase your knowledge of the people, players, processes, and procedures is a smart investment. Not only will such involvement increase your personal effectiveness, but it will also allow you to become a better mentor and supervisor.

Unrealistic expectations for other units and people will create an impression of disorganization and confusion on the part of the unit budget manager. Every budget manager, at some time, needs to ask for an exception to a rule to meet an emergency situation. But when requests for exceptions become the rule and your expectation is that your problem is more important than anyone can imagine, you are in trouble. For example, in order to pay a pending bill, you need to have a transfer made from one account to another by noon tomorrow. You just realized the problem this morning, and you ask for an exception to the five-day rule for transfers to clear. As an exception, staff in the budget and controller's office work with you to clear the transfer and make the payment on time. If, however, such last-minute requests are routine from your unit, people will be much less likely always to extend themselves to solve your problem. Unrealistic expectations for service arise from a sense of entitlement about how important you and your unit are to the institution. Keeping your sense of importance in perspective is extremely important.

Remember you do not have all the answers and if you believe that you do, you are in deep trouble as a budget manager. New budget managers, in particular, should contemplate that their new role involves different skills and competencies than they have used in the past. Seeking help is not a sign of weakness but is instead an indication of developing management maturity.

A wise budget manager also recognizes that there are many times that they will be wrong and that their projections, assessments, and plans will not turn out exactly as they expected. A good unit budget manager can provide their best thinking, but they cannot predict the future. Awareness of your own limitations and those of the system is an important part of being effective in the budget management role.

Finally, a unit budget manager is not a lone actor. An effective unit budget manager works in partnership with others across the institution and within the unit to both identify and solve problems.

REFERENCE

Barr, M. J., and Golseth, A. E. "Managing Change in a Paradoxical Environment." In M. J. Barr, M. L. Upcraft, and Associates, *New Futures for Student Affairs.* San Francisco: Jossey-Bass, 1990.

Dealing with Budget Cuts

BUDGET CUTS bring unique challenges to the academic budget manager primarily because the budget is so personnel driven. Budget reductions can occur for a variety of reasons within a college or university. Whatever the reason for the budget cut, however, being an academic budget manager in times of budget reductions is not an easy task. So when a directive comes to reduce expenditures by 5 or 10 percent, the academic budget manager will necessarily be dealing with people.

This chapter is designed to help academic budget managers with the difficult task of dealing with budget cuts. It begins with a discussion of the common reasons for budget reductions in American higher education. The chapter then focuses on institutional approaches to budget reductions. The chapter concludes with some strategies to assist the unit budget manager deal with the difficult task of budget reductions.

REASONS FOR BUDGET CUTS

Budget reductions in institutions of higher education can be caused by a number of factors. The importance of each factor will vary from institution to institution.

Lower Enrollment

For many small, private (independent) institutions, a relatively small change in enrollment can make the difference between meeting revenue targets or failing to do so. In larger institutions, the immediate impact of an enrollment reduction can be absorbed. But a long-term trend of reduced enrollment in the total institution will have adverse effects on the budget. A revenue reduction may be directly related to reduced tuition dollars or to formula-diminished funding provided to the public institution by the state.

In addition, if an institution has relied on certain academic programs as major sources of revenue, reductions in program enrollment can result in budget cuts. For example, for many years executive M.B.A. programs have provided a lucrative income stream for both the business school and the institution. In fact, the excess revenue over expenses is split on a fifty-fifty basis and amounted to almost a $1 million a year at its peak. Enrollment in the program, however, has been on a downward trajectory for the last five years and now stands at only 50 percent of the highest year of enrollment. Under these circumstances, the executive M.B.A. program, the business school, and the institution will all probably experience budget reductions.

Finally, competition for the pool of traditional-aged undergraduate students and nontraditional students can be a factor in enrollment declines. To illustrate, whereas only a few institutions offered executive M.B.A. programs in the past, that instructional option is now available at many institutions. As another example, many community colleges are offering affordable and attractive technological training in two-year programs to many potential four-year traditional-aged college students interested in technology. Enrollment shifts such as these can influence both the budget of the community college and the traditional four-year institution.

Reductions in Governmental Funding

Government funding comes to the institution in many forms, both direct and indirect. Student financial aid is a prime source of indirect government funding. When it is not increased to meet rising costs or is reduced at either the federal or state level the burden shifts to the institution, and that can cause a very great budget imbalance.

Direct sources of aid are many and have a huge influence on the fiscal health of the institution. As previously stated, comprehensive institutions of higher education rely on governmental funding for research activities and for some capital projects. When budget reductions occur at both the state and federal levels, the amount of money left to trickle down to institutions is sharply reduced. Reductions in government funding can also occur because priorities change, particularly in the research arena. Funds that used to be available to support one kind of research are diverted to other priorities because of changing circumstances or changing politics.

Finally, loss of political influence on the part of the institution can cause a reduction in government funding. If the institution has had a powerful legislative advocate at either the federal or state level and that person leaves office, then the funding circumstances of the institution are also likely to change.

Lack of Success in Fund-Raising

As noted earlier, many independent institutions rely on annual fund-raising efforts as a major source of support for both the operating budget and the endowment. If economic times change or interests of major donors are captured elsewhere, then there is a very real reduction in the funds available to operate the institution. Fund-raising is an ongoing activity for many institutions, and lack of success in that arena over multiple years will result in budget reductions.

Cutting Out of Fat

Some institutions periodically cut budgets by some factor (1 or 2 percent) on the premise that extra dollars creep into the budget through normal budgeting procedures and processes. The amount of money recaptured through such periodic budget cuts is then banked at a central institutional level. This pot of money can then be used for new and innovative ventures or as a reserve held for reductions in other funding sources.

Unusual and Costly Events

Flooding, mud slides, tornadoes, hurricanes, and other natural disasters can wreak havoc on any institutional budget and result in budget reductions for the foreseeable future. Even if the umbrella coverage insurance of the institution is available, when a major natural disaster hits losses are often in the millions of dollars. Institutional recovery from a natural disaster is a time-consuming and costly process and has an immediate budgetary impact.

Other unusual events might include legal judgments against the institution, faulty construction resulting in injuries, or liability claims against the institution. If the result is unfavorable to the institution and even if insurance is present, the initial dollar loss is a direct charge to the budget of the institution.

Another example is the massive changes in electrical rates and supply due to deregulation in both an unusual and costly event that affected most institutions in California during 2000–2001. Rising costs of fuel due to production drops in OPEC nations will have a very real effect on institutional budgets and may result in budget reductions. Unexpected rises in health care premiums, postal rates, and insurance costs can also affect budgets negatively. There are many unusual causes for institutional budget reduction.

In addition to the causes for budget reductions, unit budget managers should also understand the strategies available to the institution to implement a budget reduction.

INSTITUTIONAL APPROACHES TO BUDGET REDUCTIONS

The institution has several alternatives available when implementing a budget cut. Three issues will influence the strategy chosen: time, information, and risk tolerance.

First, how much time is available to institute cost savings measures and budget cuts? That is a critical question, for if the reduction must be made in the current operating year the strategies used will be entirely different than if the institution has two or three years to deal with a fiscal problem. It must be clear when reductions will have to be made. If a careful plan can be implemented over several years, the results will be much less painful than if the reduction must be made in the current operating budget. Unfortunately, most often academic budget managers must respond quickly to the institutional fiscal problem.

Second, just how reliable is the information available to decision makers? Decision makers must test the assumptions for a budget cut and have assurances that the decision data are reliable. Questions should be asked about past performance and future projections, and those questions should be asked in detail. Unit budget managers will probably be asked to provide some of these data and should do so in an honest and straightforward way. Reliable data from competent managers are needed to determine the scope of any necessary budget cuts.

Finally, what is the tolerance for risk within the institution? If in the long-term investment in technology will improve student services (and perhaps student reenrollment and retention), should the institution take the risk of investing in cutting-edge technology when funding is in peril? Toleration for risk will have great influence on the budget reduction strategy chosen by the institution.

Each institution will choose an institutional budget reduction strategy that is unique to that environment. Institutions of higher education commonly employ the following budget reduction strategies.

Freeze

A budget freeze is not really a budget cut, but it is perceived as one by staff members in the trenches. Under a budget freeze, new hires are stopped and major purchases are postponed. It is often used as an interim step while decision makers are trying to determine the best course of action. A budget freeze is also a good way to get the attention of faculty and staff regarding the serious nature of the institutional financial problem at the institution.

Across-the-Board Cuts

Use of across-the-board cuts is the easiest, most expedient way to manage a budget reduction. Unit budget managers are simply informed that they must cut X percent from their budget and must report the cuts to the central budget office. The money recovered from these measures will be used to offset financial problems within the institution or as a tool to avoid deficit spending in the current fiscal year. An across-the-board cut provides great flexibility for unit budget managers regarding where cuts should be made. It is equitable in one sense, since all units within the institution are treated alike. It does not differentiate, however, between units that have more flexibility in their budgets and those that are already operating in tight fiscal circumstances. The impact of across-the-board cuts is thus felt differentially within the institution.

Targeted Reductions

Another institutional strategy is to select certain line items or certain units for targeted reductions and savings. This reduces flexibility at the unit level but may provide a more equitable approach to implementing reductions between units. Examples might include targeting travel, honoraria, and the purchase of all equipment. All funds associated with these line items will be then held centrally, and units will need to demonstrate a special case to spend any of those funds.

Targeted reductions also involve the search for new funds to support essential institutional services. The unit budget manager will need to have good evaluative data to justify the need for unit programs or they may become targets for budget reductions.

Restructuring

A more draconian measure is restructuring the way the institution does business through combining programs, instituting new fiscal measures, and investing in technology for long-term gains in efficiency and effectiveness. Restructuring can be a painful and difficult process and because people are involved it is fraught with emotions. What programs should be combined? Who should stay and who should go? Restructuring can, however, result in substantial savings through reduction in administrative overhead.

New fiscal measures such as reducing the time for payments, greater return on investment of cash balances, and improving internal processes so that cash reserves are not used for operations can all help capture substantial savings. The keys to successful implementation of any new fiscal measures is timing and explanation of why the change is being made.

As noted earlier, technology investments represent a risk but they also hold great potential for improving financial systems. Investing in technology may be an expense in the short run, but if the system is carefully chosen it may be a method to speed processes and thus improve cash flow.

Whatever the choice of institutional strategy, there are a number of actions that a unit budget manager can take to institute budget reductions in the most humane and fairest ways possible.

USEFUL UNIT STRATEGIES

Since unit budgets in higher education are often personnel intensive, budget reductions usually involve people. In a time of retrenchment either their jobs or the programs they care about are in jeopardy. When budget reductions occur, morale is a key issue to confront. Some strategies that can be used to meet budget reduction targets in the most humane way possible include the following:

Share Information

Rumors will abound when budget reductions are announced. The gossip lines will be working overtime within the department and on the campus. One of the most useful ways to aid colleagues is to provide information to them about what is happening in as clear a fashion as possible. Even if you do not yet know what is going on, let them know that. Trust is then reinforced and people, at least, feel that they are being kept informed. When you do know the strategy being employed by the institution, share that information in as clear and concise way as possible.

Ask for Suggestions

There are a lot of good ideas within the unit and now is the time to ask for help and suggestions from your colleagues. In what ways do they think money can be saved or reductions made? What are their ideas? Even if their ideas cannot be implemented, they will have had an opportunity to be heard.

Use Contingency Funds First

Earlier in this volume, the suggestion was made to build a contingency line into your budget. It may be labeled as a contingency or it may be a line item such as equipment replacement that can be postponed. Whenever possible the unit budget should always try to include such flexible funds in the unit budget or through the development of reserve funds. Such funds should be the first source to be tapped to meet targeted budget reductions.

Ask for Voluntary Cutbacks

If members of the unit understand the dimensions of the problem, they can come up with solutions that you have not even thought of. Sometimes your colleagues will surprise you with their creativity and willingness to contribute. There may be people within the unit, for instance, that actually would welcome a ten-month appointment as opposed to a twelve-month appointment. There may be others who would like to reduce their status from full-time to three–quarter time. Listen to all of these proposals carefully and honor the sentiments behind them.

In addition, staff colleagues may come up with gestures that will not save a great deal of money but are symbolic of their commitment to helping confront the issue. Charging for office coffee when it had been provided at no charge is one such example. Voluntary reductions only succeed as a solution when everyone understands the gravity of the situation.

Make Few Promises

No unit budget manager fully understands the complexity of the financial issues being faced on an institutional level. Budget reductions are a time when you should make few promises and only make promises you will be sure you can honor. Your credibility is on the line and, in tough times, that is one of the few "coins of the realm" that you have. Promise support, provide information, but never say "never" when asked the question of whether a person will lose his or her job.

Cut Back on Nonessentials

Every budget has nonessential items that are not central to the core of the enterprise. A very first step in managing budget reductions at the unit level is to identify and reduce financial commitments to nonessential items. Do you really need a poster-making machine? Is it necessary for all computers to be upgraded in one year? Is recarpeting needed now or can it be put off for a time? Is new office furniture necessary? Ask the hard questions and target those items that would be nice but are not essential.

Consider Outsourcing

Outsourcing, or hiring contract services, for certain functions may be a means to reduce the unit budget. Dickeson (1999) provides a helpful list of questions to assist a budget manager in determining whether outsourcing is a viable budget reduction strategy. Such a change should not be entered into lightly, as it is a long-term approach to financial problem solving. This option should be carefully discussed with decision makers even prior to soliciting information from vendors.

Share Resources

With careful planning it may be possible to reduce the budget by sharing resources with another unit. Equipment is often the easiest commodity to share. For example, if offices are in close proximity a shared fax machine or copier is a real possibility. In addition, with the right office configuration positions might be shared with reception and initial phone responses for two offices being combined into one position. There are many possibilities. Think creatively with your colleagues and new solutions may be found.

Be Consistent

Consistency has been an ongoing theme in this volume, and it is essential to unit budget manager success. For if you are not consistent in what you say or do, then your credibility is at stake and managing in difficult circumstances becomes even more complicated.

In times of uncertainty (which are by definition times of budget reductions), information will constantly change. As a unit budget manager, you need to consistently transmit those changing messages to those in your department and then help them interpret what they might mean. Your fairness and consistency will go a long way in bringing stability to difficult decisions.

Don't Be Afraid to Make Difficult Decisions

When all else fails, you must be prepared to make difficult decisions. Termination of employees is never easy, and it is much more difficult when the termination is caused by forces outside the control of the manager. Develop a rationale that will hold up to scrutiny for the difficult decision. Seek advice from both human resources and legal counsel if employees will be affected by the decision. Finally, you must take responsibility for the decision within the context of the circumstances that you are dealing with at the time. Although you did not cause the need for the budget reduction, you did make the decision of the position(s) to be eliminated or reduced. That is your management role, and it is a difficult but necessary one (Exhibit 5.1).

Summary

Dealing with budget reduction is never an easy task for a unit budget manager. In most cases, however, the process of how the budget manager approaches the issue of reductions is very important. A fair, impartial, and

---

Exhibit 5.1. Budget Reduction Strategies That Work.

1. Let people within the unit know what is going on and solicit their suggestions.
2. Look first to contingency funds as a source to capture needed dollars.
3. Inquire whether or not anyone is willing to make a voluntary cutback in time or compensation.
4. Make few promises, for you do not control the entire situation.
5. Identify and reduce the nonessential items in the budget.
6. Embrace symbolic gestures that reinforce the commitment to solving budget problems.
7. Be consistent in what you say and do.
8. Consider outsourcing some functions within the unit.
9. Share or combine resources with other units.
10. Have the courage to honestly make the difficult decisions.

open approach reduces anxiety among colleagues and helps them understand the realities that are facing the institution and the unit.

Budget reductions are not the time to pull back from interactions with colleagues but rather are times for sharing and soliciting their feedback and concerns. For example, sometimes you will uncover a misperception that is shared across the institution and can be easily corrected by additional information.

In the end, however, a unit budget manager must not be afraid to make the hard decisions necessary to meet institutional expectations for budget reductions.

THE FINAL WORD

Sound financial management at all levels of the institution is essential for institutional success. Every level of the organization must pay careful attention to budgeting and financial issues because the institution's financial health only reflects the aggregate financial health of the individual units that make up the whole. Unit budget managers can make a difference not only within their unit but in the institution as a whole. In order to do so you must invest time and energy in your role as a unit budget manager. Your problems and dilemmas are not much different from those faced by the president of Alpha University (outlined earlier in this volume). They differ only in the amount of money involved and the complexity of the issues involved. Managing the fiscal resources of your unit in an effective and efficient manner can be rewarding work, for it does make a difference. The budget development process provides a unique opportunity for a unit to articulate goals, aspirations, and priorities and link them to the academic mission of the institution. Further, budget development helps the unit more clearly understand its mission within the larger context of the institution.

As a unit budget manager you will also fill an important role in translating the financial decisions made at the institution to your colleagues within your unit. Such translation is serious and important work and can help create a common bond of shared goals within the institution.

Good budgeting and financial management requires attention to detail, a curious mind, and a willingness to persist while seeking answers to questions. The skills of budgeting can be learned if the task is approached with low ego involvement and a willingness to find out what you do not know.

REFERENCES

Dickeson, R.C. *Prioritizing Academic Services and Programs: Reallocating Resources to Achieve Strategic Balance.* San Francisco: Jossey-Bass, 1999.

GLOSSARY OF TERMS

Appropriation. The amount of money transferred to the institution by action of the state or federal government. It can also mean the amount of money allocated to a budget unit within the institution.

Auxiliary enterprise. A unit of the institution that must generate sufficient income to pay all operating expenses (including institutional overhead) and fund long-term repair and maintenance of facilities and equipment.

Budget unit. A budget unit may be a large program, a department, or a division of the institution.

Capital budget. The current fiscal year financial plan for funding revenue and expenses for items that will benefit the institution longer than one fiscal year. Examples include facilities, infrastructure, vehicles, furniture, and equipment.

Encumbrance. An accounting entry that "saves" money to cover an expense that extends over more than one accounting period in the fiscal year. For example, salaries are usually encumbered for the year and the encumbered funds are used to pay the salary each month.

Endowment. The long-term assets of the institution that are invested for future growth and support of the institution. Use of the endowment is usually limited to all or a portion of the income generated from investment of the endowment corpus.

Fees for services. Fees paid by students and others for access to services beyond those included in tuition charges, such as fees for psychological services after an initial therapy period or fees for health care beyond an initial diagnosis period.

Fiscal year. A twelve-month period, designated by the institution, for fiscal activity. Most commonly in higher education, the fiscal year begins either on July 1 and closes on June 30 or it begins on September 1 and closes on August 31.

Fungible money. Funds that are not restricted and can be moved from one purpose to another within the institutional budget.

Indirect costs. A charge in a grant or contract designed to repay the institution (in part) for institutional services and facilities provided for the grant.

Incremental budgeting. A budgeting system whereby the budget for the current fiscal year becomes the base for an incremental allocation for the next fiscal year.

Line item. A specific category of expenses within an operating budget of the institution or a unit. Examples include postage, telephone, office supplies, and the like. Sometimes classified as an object code.

Mandatory fees. A fee that must be paid by all students in a certain category such as all full-time undergraduate students or all full-time graduate students.

Nonmandatory fees. Fees that may be paid by a student for access to certain services or events but are not required to be paid by all students.

Operating budget. The financial plan for revenue and expenses of the institution for the current fiscal year.

Outsourcing. Contracting with an outside vendor for a service formerly provided by institutional personnel.

Overhead. The amount of money charged by the institution to auxiliary enterprises, self-supporting units, and grants to recover the costs for general institutional expenses such as accounting, campus police, and budget support.

Redistribution. Reallocating funds from one line item to another within the total budget allocation.

Reserve accounts. Accounts that are funded by budget units and are permitted to accrue dollars from year to year. Reserve accounts are used to fund capital projects or deal with unusual fiscal circumstances faced by a unit.

Zero-based budgeting. The operating budget is developed from scratch each year and is based on projected revenues and the level of service to be provided in the various units of the institution. Every line item expense and revenue source must be justified each year.

SUGGESTIONS FOR FURTHER READING

Balderston, F. E. *Managing Today's University* (2nd. ed.). San Francisco: Jossey-Bass, 1995.

Brinkman, P. T. "Formula Budgeting: The Fourth Decade." In L. Leslie (ed.), *Responding to New Realities in Funding.* New Directions for Institutional Research, no. 43. San Francisco: Jossey-Bass, 1984.

Bryson, J. M. *Strategic Planning for Public and Non-Profit Organizations.* San Francisco: Jossey-Bass, 1998.

Dickeson, R. C. *Prioritizing Academic Programs and Services: Reallocating Resources to Achieve Strategic Balance.* San Francisco: Jossey-Bass, 1999.

Flawn, P. T. *A Primer for University Presidents: Managing the Modern University.* Austin: The University of Texas Press, 1990.

Higher Education Surveys. *The Finances of Higher Education Institutions.* Higher Education Survey Report Number Eight, November. Sponsored by the National Science Foundation, the National Endowment for the Humanities and the United States Department of Education, 1990.

Maddox, D. *Budgeting for Not-For-Profit Organizations.* New York: Wiley, 1999.

McIlnay, D. P. *How Foundations Work: What Grant Seekers Need to Know About the Many Faces of Foundations.* San Francisco: Jossey-Bass, 1998.

Meisinger R. J., and Dubeck, L. W. *College and University Budgeting: An Introduction for Faculty and Academic Administrators.* Washington, D.C.: National Association of College and University Business Officers, 1984.

National Commission on the Cost of Higher Education (1988). *Straight Talk About College Costs and Prices.* Washington, D.C.: American Council on Education, 1998.

Scott, D. L. *Wall Street Words.* Boston: Houghton Mifflin, 1988.

Shim, J. K., and Siegel, J. *Financial Management for Non-Profits.* New York: McGraw Hill, 1997.

Taylor, B. E., and Massey, W. F. *Strategic Indicators for Higher Education.* Princeton, N.J.: Peterson's, 1996.

Upcraft, M. L., and Barr, M. J. (eds.) *Managing Student Affairs Effectively.* New Directions for Student Services, no. 43. San Francisco: Jossey-Bass, 1988.

Woodard, D. B. Jr., and von Destinon, M. "Budgeting and Fiscal Management." In M. J. Barr, M. K. Desler, and Associates, *The Handbook of Student Affairs Administration.* (2nd. ed.). San Francisco: Jossey-Bass, 2000.

Yeager, J. L., Nelson, G. M., Potter, E. A., Weidman, J. C., and Zullo, T. G. (eds.) *ASHE Reader on Finance in Higher Education* (2nd ed.). Boston: Pearson Custom Publishing, 2001.

INDEX

A

Academic budget manager. *See* Unit budget manager

Access and choice issues, 30; and competition for students, 10; and cost of attendance, 8–9

Accounting statements, review of, 60–61

Adult and returning students, services for, 10–11

Animal Welfare Act (AWA), 9

Annual giving programs, 16–17

Appropriation, defined, 107

Audit requirements, 26–27

Audited report of performance, 64

Auxiliary enterprises: budgets for, 35, 55–56; and capital funds, 36; defined, 107; and reserve funds, 20, 73–74; self-sustaining nature of, 19–20, 72–73

B

Barr, M. J., 82, 83

Bond sales and rating, 37

Buckley Amendment, 9

Budget: approval process, 58–59; cost centered approach to, 42; and cost saving options, 56–57; elements of, 42–44; and forecasting, 66–67; formula approach to, 40–41; incremental, 37–38; performance monitoring

of, 60–61; PPBS (Planning, Programming, and Budgeting Systems) approach to, 40; purposes of, 30–34; redistribution in, 38–39; responsibility centered approach to, 41–42; types of, 35–37; zero-based, 39–40

Budget committee, 53

Budget cuts, 95–106; across-the-board, 99–100; and budget freeze, 99; common reasons for, 95–98; and government funding, 96–97; and institutional strategies, 98–101; and outsourcing, 103; and restructuring, 100–101; and targeted reductions, 100; unit strategies for, 101–4; and unusual/costly events, 97–98; and voluntary cutbacks, 102

Budget development: centralized approach to, 32–33, 44–45; expense prediction in, 43–44; goals and priorities in, 4–5, 30–31, 71–72; hidden cost considerations in, 84–85; hybrid approach to, 33, 46; information sharing in, 53; internal process for, 53; models, 37–42; revenue identification and classification in, 42–43; timetables, 52; unit-based approach to, 33, 45–46, 52–58

Budget documents: as communication tools, 33–34; preparation and submission of, 67

Budget forecasting, 66–67
Budget guidelines and rules, 50–52
Budget manager. *See* Unit budget
  manager
Budget office, defined, 3–4
Budget proposals: assumptions made
  in, 92; review of, 54–57
Budget reduction strategies, 98–105
Budget reports: audited financial, 64;
  monthly review of, 60–61
Budget review, 34
Budget unit, defined, 3
Budget year, closing dates in, 62–63

C

Capital budget, 36–37; cost estimate for,
  70–71; defined, 107; and final project
  approval, 71–72; financial plan in,
  69–70, 72; and preliminary project
  review, 70; priorities in, 71–72;
  process, 67–72; program statements
  for, 68–69; source of funds for, 67
Capital expenses: definition of, 36; and
  outsourcing, 21; state and federal
  appropriations for, 21–22, 97; and
  sale of bonds, 37
Cash budget, 35
Central budget office: advice and input
  from, 81–82; defined, 4; and endowment income, 16; and gamemanship
  strategies, 90; and large fund expenditures, 33
Centralized model of budget development, 32–33, 44–45
Communication, as budget function,
  33–34
Constituency groups, and budget
  process, 89
Contingency funds, and budget cuts,
  101–2
Contract review, legal advice in, 90
Contracted institutional services, 21;
  as revenue source, 19, 32
Cost of attendance: and financial aid,
  8–9; and student fee increases,
  5, 8

Cost of goods and services: budgeting
  approach to, 44; increase in, 11–12
Cost–centered budgeting, 40

D

Development office, 2
Dickeson, R. C., 56
Discrete fund sources, 42–43
Discretionary costs, 44
Diversity: and competition for students,
  10–11; and student financial aid
  issues, 8–9
Doctoral programs, institutional costs
  of, 14
Dubeck, L. W., 35

E

Encumbrance, defined, 107
Endowments: defined, 107; fiduciary
  management of, 16–17
Expense budget, 43–44

F

Faculty compensation: guidelines,
  25–26; operating budget and, 35
Faculty recruitment and retention,
  9–10
Family Education Rights and Privacy Act
  (FERPA), 9
Federal funding: for capital projects,
  22; reductions in, 96–97; and regulations, 9
Federal research grants, 19
Fees for service, 16, 27; defined, 107
Financial aid budgets, 8, 10
Financial plan, 69–70
Fiscal environment: capital expenses and
  funding in, 21–22; and competitive
  environment of higher education,
  7–11; cost concerns in, 11–12; and
  funding sources, 12–24; grants and
  contracts in, 18–19; overview of,
  7–12; in public versus private institutions, 22–28; regulations in, 9;

tuition and student fees in, 5, 8, 13–16. *See also* Fund-raising; State funding

Fiscal management: assessment of financial capabilities in, 80; of bond sales and debt repayment, 37; and budget manager's attitude, 92–93; budgeting strategies for, 32; centralized model for, 32–33; and change strategy, 82; and endowment income, 16–17; ethics in, 82–83, 91; game playing in, 89–90, *91*; inappropriate strategies in, 89; and institutional guidelines and practices, 86; and multiyear consequences, 85–86; organizational culture and, 79; pitfalls and problems in, 2–3, 77–94; principle of establishing commonality in, 82; problem identification and problem solving in, 80–82, 84; and revenue estimates, 83–84; suggestions for success in, 87–92; utility principle in, 83; unit-centered model of, 33

Fiscal policies, in public versus private institutions, 25

Fiscal year, 35–36, 108; budget phases of, 49–67

Formula budgeting, 13, 40–41

Funding sources, 12–24; budgeting process and, 42–43; federal, 19, 22, 96–97; one-time, 42; for public versus private institutions, 22–24; state, 7–8, 21–22; and variable income, 43

Fund-raising, 2; and annual giving programs, 17–18; and budget reductions, 97; and long-term campaigns, 18

Fungible money, defined, 108

G

Golseth, A. E., 82, 83

Goods and services, and purchasing regulations, 26

Governing board, and budget review and approval process, 34, 58–59

Government funding reductions, 96–97

Graduate education programs, 9

Graduate tuition, institutional costs of, 14

Grant(s), 8, 67; closing of, 85; proposal, 19, 58; as revenue sources, 18–19, 32

H

Higher Education Price Index, 38

Human resources: and operating budget, 35; in public versus private institutions, 25–26

Human Subjects Research Act, 9

I

Incremental budget, 37–38; defined, 108; model, 51

Indirect costs, defined, 108

Inflationary cost increases, 55–56

Institutional oversight, in public versus private institutions, 25

Internal audit, 26–27

L

Legal consultation, in contract review, 90–91

Legislative budget process, 13

Line item expenses: defined, 108; review of, 13

M

Maddox, D. C., 30, 32, 38, 44

Mandatory fees, defined, 108

Mayhew, L. B., 29, 33

Meisinger, R. J., 35

Minority student enrollments, 10

Multiple year fiscal consequences, 85–86

Multiyear plan, 32, 75

N

New budget managers: advice for, 87–92; and attitudinal issues, 92–94; and common budget issues and problems, 77–87

Nonmandatory fees, defined, 108
Nontraditional students, and new service demands, 10–11

O

Occupational Safety and Health Act of 1970 (OSHA), 9
One–time fund sources, 15–16, 42
Operating budget: adjustment of, 61–62; analysis of, 63–66; building flexibility into, 86–87; and cash budget, 35; closing of, 62–63; defined, 35, 108; development phases of, 49–67; and fiscal year variance, 35–36; inflationary cost increases and, 55–56; typical unit cycle of, 65
Outsourcing: and budget cuts, 103; concept of, 21
Overhead, defined, 108

P

Personnel: budgeting for, 43, 51; and legal consultation, 90; and regulatory requirements, 26. *See also* Human resources
Planning, Programming, and Budgeting Systems (PPBS) model, 40
Prioritizing Academic Programs and Services (Dickeson), 56
Private institutions: church-related, 21; endowment support for, 16–17; fiscal policies in, 25; funding control and approval in, 25; human resource issues in, 25–26; and mandatory student fees, 15; and sharing of budget information, 34; state funding for, 8; tuition in, 14
Professional school programs, institutional costs of, 14
Program enrollment, and budget cuts, 96
Program initiatives, prioritization of, 56
Program statements, 68–69
Public institutions: and capital budget funding, 36–37; compensation guidelines in, 25–26; and constituency communication, 33–34; and endow-

ment income, 17; funding oversight in, 25; state funding for, 7–8, 13–14
Purchasing regulations, 26

R

Recruitment costs, 9–11
Redistribution: defined, 108; process, 38–38
Regulatory requirements: financial implications of, 9; and personnel matters, 26; in purchasing of goods and services, 26
Required/fixed costs, 44
Research Associates of Washington, 38
Research funding, 9, 97
Reserve accounts, 32; and auxiliary enterprises, 20, 73–74; defined, 109
Resource allocation, and needs versus wants, 31–32
Responsibility centered budgeting, 41–42
Restructuring, and institutional budget cuts, 100–101
Revenue estimates, 83–84
Revenue shortfalls, 61–62
Revenue targets, enrollment and, 95–96
Rooney, P. M., 42

S

Schuh, J., 7
Special programs, institutional funding for, 20
Staff compensation: guidelines, 25–26; operating budget and, 35
Staff recruitment and retention, 9–10
Stakeholders, identification of, 88
State audits, 27
State funding: for capital improvements, 21–22; and formula budgeting, 13, 40–41; process, 13; reductions in, 7–8, 96–97
State regulations, 9
Stocum, D. L., 42
Student enrollment, and budget cuts, 96
Student fees: increases in, 5, 8; manda-

tory, 15; one-time and fees for service, 15–16; as revenue source, 15–16

Student financial aid, and government funding reductions, 96–97

Student recruitment and retention costs, 10–11

Student Right-to-Know and Campus Security Act, 9

T

Technology, 36; and competition for faculty and staff, 10; fiscal impact of, 11; investments, 31–32, 100–101

Tuition: as funding source, 13–14; statutory restrictions on, 14

U

Undergraduate tuition, as funding source, 13–14

Unions, and human resource issues, 26

Unit budget manager, 1–3; and analysis of budget performance, 63–66; and capital budget, 67–68; decentralized approach and, 33; defined, 3; and development of budget requests, 52–58;

fiscal management role of, 2, 93; forecasting and, 66–67; fund raising and, 2; as institutional listening post, 2; problem-solving role of, 2–3

Unit budget(s): and institutional parameters, 50–52; internal guidelines/timetables for, 54; members' involvement in, 53–54; process, 53; and previous budgets, 52

Unit operating budget, 44

Unit-based budgeting, *12,* 45–46; and responsibility centered budgeting, 41–42

V

von Destinon, M., 35, 41, 53

W

Wachtel, E., 83

Woodard, D. B., Jr., 35, 41, 53

Z

Zero-based budgeting: defined, 109; model, 39–40, 43